TRUE TALES OF THE SOUTH AT WAR

How Soldiers Fought and Families Lived
1861–1865

Collected and Edited by

Clarence Poe

with

Betsy Seymour

DOVER PUBLICATIONS, INC.
New York

Published in Canada by General Publishing Company, Ltd., 30 Lesmill Road, Don Mills, Toronto, Ontario.

Published in the United Kingdom by Constable and Company, Ltd., 3 The Lanchesters, 162–164 Fulham Palace Road, London W6 9ER.

Bibliographical Note

This Dover edition, first published in 1995, is an unabridged and unaltered republication of the work originally published in 1961 by The University of North Carolina Press, Chapel Hill.

Library of Congress Cataloging-in-Publication Data

True tales of the South at war : how soldiers fought and families lived, 1861–1865 / collected and edited by Clarence Poe with Betsy Seymour. — Dover ed.
    p.   cm.
Originally published: Chapel Hill : University of North Carolina Press, 1961.
Includes index.
ISBN 0-486-28451-4 (pbk.)
  1. United States—History—Civil War, 1861–1865—Personal narratives, Confederate. 2. Confederate States of America—History—Sources. I. Poe, Clarence Hamilton, 1881–   . II. Seymour, Betsy.
E605.T77   1995
973.7'82—dc20   94-34997
                                                                          CIP

Manufactured in the United States of America
Dover Publications, Inc., 31 East 2nd Street, Mineola, N.Y. 11501

*This volume is dedicated
to one large group I would especially honor
and to the memory of
a soldier-father and a soldier-son—*

To ALL MEN AND WOMEN

who share the rich heritage of descent
from, or kinship with, any of the heroic
men and women who served in one
of the world's greatest wars, 1861-1865.

To WILLIAM BAXTER POE, 1839-1907,

who had opposed secession but, when
he thought his state unconstitutionally
invaded, served the Confederacy until
its final downfall.

To WILLIAM DISMUKES POE, 1915-1958,

who hated all war, but to help prevent
the threatened world-domination of
Hitlerism, served with the forces of
Freedom in World War II until their
final victory.

Foreword

WALTER PAGE ONCE SAID, "I WISH I COULD HAVE THIS AS MY epitaph: 'Here Lies the Man Who Killed the Preface!'"

Nevertheless may we not reasonably say that every prospective reader is entitled to ask about any book, "Who wrote it, why and how?" Such questions about this volume I shall now try to answer.

I am myself the son of a Confederate soldier-farmer who survived the War—I am named for a Confederate who did not survive—and for sixty years have tried to preserve significant memories and documents of Southerners in war—in my youth for several years as secretary and later president of our state historical association and ever since as an editor and individual. I have talked with Confederates who saw Sumter fired on and with others who drank with Lee the bitter dregs of defeat at Appomattox. More importantly, a year ago after I made an appeal to 1,400,000 subscribing families to *The Progressive Farmer* magazine, hundreds of persons from Maryland to Texas inclusive sent me valuable Civil War letters, diaries, and reminiscences with heartwarming expressions of a desire to help me. (And having now uttered the words "Civil War," let me explain that I do so because it is now so generally accepted in all sections and because it represents a pleasant retreat on the part of our Northern friends from their original official phrase, "The War of the Rebellion.")

My almost lifelong effort to preserve war memories I have made because of these three strong convictions: (1) if your grandfather or any other kinsman served in the Civil War then he fought in a war as great and historic as any ever waged by Caesar, Alexander, Hannibal, or Napoleon; (2) that so competent a student and writer of history as Theodore Roosevelt was right when he said, "The world has never seen better soldiers than those who followed Lee," and (3) that this war was sustained by women no less heroic than the men.

Another compelling reason for my interest in studying and preserving our war history is that (born in January, 1881) I grew up with Confederate soldiers all around me, and kept up my contacts and interest as long as any lived. My earliest recollections are of words associated with my father's war service—Seven Pines, Petersburg, Fredericksburg, Pocataligo, Charleston—and gangrene! My mother's interest centered in Vicksburg because there her only brother and four Mississippi cousins endured one of the most appalling and soul-testing sieges our New World has ever known. And what a rare privilege it was when I once heard Mrs. Stonewall Jackson talk of her hero husband when I spent an evening with her at the home of her granddaughter—and another evening I spent with the widow of General William D. Pender (killed at Gettysburg at age 29, the youngest major general in the Confederate Army) who was herself a cousin of my mother's.

And so this volume came into being. Maybe it will prove to be the nearest approach to the book the mythical Southern scholar wanted to see—*An Impartial History of The Civil War—Written From the Southern Point of View!* It is at any rate a book by Southerners themselves—about soldiers who did the doing, daring, and dying at the front, the wives and others who kept the home fires burning, the children and grandchildren who later heard the stories of the old folks. Much of it is first hand—letters written on the battlefield or in prison or hospital, diaries of day to day life behind the lines. Some of it is second and third hand (but with credibility scrupulously considered)—and though such material may seem less valuable to the historian, I think stories and local traditions may be as true to the *spirit* of these stirring times as first-hand documents.

Certainly we have attempted no comprehensive report on all aspects of the war. Especially have we left to others all biographies of famous leaders, the grand strategy of generals, the maneuvers of vast armies. Instead there are just two sentences which may well be remembered as the keynotes of our effort. One is Tennyson's line based on the universal appeal of tales since the days of Aesop, Homer and Chaucer—"And truth embodied in a tale shall enter in at lowly doors," and Macaulay's sentence regarding his *History of England:* "I shall cheerfully bear the reproach of having descended below the dignity of [conventional] history if I can succeed in placing before the English of the nineteenth century a true picture of the life of their ancestors."

It is such a "true picture" of Civil War days in the South that we hope comes through in the multi-varied true tales in this volume. And it is our belief that such a true picture will indeed help men and women, North and South, to honor all those on either side "who fought for the right as God gave them to see the right."

CLARENCE POE

Raleigh, N.C.

Acknowledgments

FEW AUTHORS HAVE EVER HAD SUCH GENEROUS HELP AS I HAVE had in preparing this volume. First of all I thank all the hundreds of correspondents whose contributions made it possible. To the gifted and indefatigable Mrs. Ralph Seymour who has so capably worked with me in the selection and compilation of material, I am especially grateful, and to my untiring secretary, Mrs. Ruth C. Reynolds. Especially heartening have been the generous interest and encouragement of my associates on *The Progressive Farmer*. Next I would thank numerous county historians, officers of historical societies, and editors of local newspapers. The following persons who have generously given me permission to use the indicated portions of this book have my gratitude: for the Colonel L. L. Polk letters, Miss Leonita Denmark and Mr. L. Polk Denmark; for selections from Mrs. Edmonston's diary, the North Carolina Department of Archives and History (which will later print the diary in full); for Miss Mordecai's diary, Mr. Rudolph Turk; for the Berry Benson chapter, Mr. Charles Benson (the University of Georgia Press will print the diary in full next year). I am also much indebted to Mrs. Hunter Bourne of Virginia for bringing Mrs. McGuire's diary to my attention, and other helpful interest.

Especial thanks also are due to the librarian of the University of North Carolina and Mr. James Patton, curator of the Southern Historical Collection there; to the staff of the North Carolina State Library and Miss Clyde Smith of the Olivia Raney Library, and to Mr. Richard Walser for many helpful suggestions. Finally, my wife, Alice Aycock Poe, and my granddaughter, Jean Poe, have helped much in reading manuscripts. Nor is it any mere case of giving an apple to the teacher when I add my thanks to the staff of the University of North Carolina Press for suggestions and constructive criticism that have been immensely helpful. In copying all old manuscripts we have sought to follow the exact wording, but have modernized spelling and punctuation.

Contents

CHAPTER ONE

The Changing Faces of War

THE CIVIL WAR WAS ONE OF THE MOST TRAGIC OF ALL WARS *because it pitted friends and brothers against one another in a nightmare of often hand-to-hand fighting. It was made more tragic, too, by the fact that since her forces were so overwhelmingly outnumbered the South's cause was hopeless from the beginning. Yet not all was horror and bloodshed; many accounts, humorous or heart-warming, have been handed down to us. And in retrospect many a Confederate soldier, such as George W. Rabb of Catawba County, N.C., actually remembered many of his wartime experiences with pleasure:*

I had many close calls, but I think the closest place I ever was in was at Spotsylvania Court House. Three of my company were killed, all within four feet of me. How I escaped, I cannot tell. I never surrendered but once; then the cavalry was over us, and one had his sword drawn to split my head. But just before he struck at me, I fell to the ground, and he hurried on; then I arose and made my escape back to our lines. . . . Notwithstanding all this, I must confess now while old, I had a lot of fun, and was lucky to lose only a leg, all of which I thank my Heavenly Father for.

1

When the Confederacy called for enlistments, thousands answered, not from a reluctant sense of duty, but enthusiastically with an exalted sense of the righteousness of their cause. Many of the wealthier were accompanied by slaves dedicated to the master's comfort and safety. Mrs. Tom Irby of Texas says:

At the beginning of the war, my father's group of volunteers, each man with his Negro body servant, mounted their horses and rode to Fayetteville, Arkansas, to enlist. As most of them were slaveowners, I suppose it did not occur to them to fight in any company that had to walk. . . .

My father was full of reminiscences of the war, but none of them conveyed any feeling of hatred toward the Northern army. He told us of the two opposing armies encamped within calling distances of each other and of how the Southern soldiers would exchange tobacco with the Yankees for food or clothing. (It seemed they never had enough clothing.) He made us laugh by his stories of how they could not sleep at night because each soldier had a small war of his own—the Northern "body-lice" battling with the Southern "cooties." He told about his Negro boy trying to run away and go back home and how he caught him and brought him back and told him he would have to spread his bed roll down beside him so he could prevent this happening again, and how horrified the Negro was at the thought of having to sleep with his master—a thought more terrifying than being shot to pieces. . . .

Another reference to the lice which still bedeviled our soldiers in two World Wars is made in the following letter from a Confederate soldier in camp near Shelbyville, Tennessee: "There are two sorts of body guards; some are men and the others are lice, and the lice are the most numerous. They are in for the duration of the war, and they never desert their command."

Although the Civil War sometimes pitted brother against brother in hatred, it often led father and son to enlist together out of their love for each other. Mrs. Ethel Harvey of Texas tells such a story:

The A. M. Boyd family was living in northeast Arkansas when war broke out. The elder son, Zack, was drafted into the Confederate army in 1864, just after his eighteenth birthday. Zack was not strong and had never been away from home. So his father decided to enlist with him in the hope of making it easier for the son, although he knew he could not make a foot soldier because he had never fully recovered from a leg injury received when he was struck by a falling tree. Mr. Boyd and Zack left home in the fall of 1864. The family never saw either again. Zack died of pneumonia brought on by exposure before recovering from measles. Mr. Boyd, serving as dispatcher, left company headquarters riding a mule to deliver a message for his commanding officer but never got through with the message.

In the earlier days of the war in both North and South unwilling draftees who could afford it hired substitutes. Mrs. Ruby Grove of Georgia gives this example: "Grandfather Neal Murphy who lived in Monroe County, Alabama, had eight children when he enlisted. Knowing he would soon be called he went in the place of a younger man who paid him $2,000 to substitute for him. He died of measles in Mobile; was never in a battle."

And sometimes a soldier would volunteer to substitute temporarily for a friend. Mrs. J. A. Shropshire of Tennessee says, "Once when a battle was pending John Roark, my uncle, had a premonition he would not come through that

*battle and related his feeling to a comrade, Bill Conner, an-
other uncle of mine. Bill took his place when his name was
called and he contended ever after that his comrade saved
his life that day."*

*The youngest substitute we know of was also one of the
youngest Confederate soldiers. He was W. D. Tranham, of
Camden, South Carolina. In a speech to other Confederate
veterans August 1, 1896, he explained why he enlisted at the
astonishing if not unprecedented age of thirteen:*

I have been frequently asked how I came to go into the
army so young. At the close of the session (King's Mountain
Military School at Yorkville) on November 11, 1860 (which
was my thirteenth birthday), I returned home, and for the
next few months read all the newspapers I could lay my
hands on, notably the Charleston Mercury and the Charleston Courier.

In January, 1861, a meeting of the young men of upper
Kershaw was called in Camden for the purpose of organiz-
ing a company of volunteers. I was not present at that meeting. But I was anxious to become a soldier and soon obtained
permission of my parents to volunteer. Having given her
consent, my mother suggested that I take the place of Mr.
William Cochrane, saying he was a poor man with a large
family who would suffer in his absence, and he ought not to
leave them. I thought the suggestion a good one, and my
father said it was "the very thing." But Mr. Cochrane refused at first to consider the proposition. He yielded, however, to argument, and Capt. Haile enrolled me in his stead,
I thus becoming the first "substitute" of the war.

When we reached Richmond, among those who met us at
the train was the venerable Edmund Ruffin who with his
flowing white locks presented a striking appearance. After a
few weeks we proceeded to Fairfax Courthouse. There for

about a month we labored on breastworks, drilled, went on picket, and did guard duty in the camp.

On July 17, the signs were ominous. Staff officers were galloping hither and thither. It was evident that an emergency was at hand. Tents were struck, the "long roll" was sounded as only Prichard could beat it, and the regiment took position in the breastworks we had constructed. In our front for more than a mile the country was open and slightly rolling. Soon the enemy, about a mile distant, marched across our front from right to left—their purpose being to turn our left flank. I shall never forget the magnificent spectacle—15,000 men splendidly uniformed and equipped, their guns glittering in the morning sunlight.

I remember well my feelings at this time. I knew we were about to go into battle and realized fully the seriousness of the situation. But I listened to those guns, and thought they made the grandest music I had ever heard!

Later in the fall of 1861, we fell back to the line of Bull Run, the 2nd regiment going into camp near Blackburn's Ford. About this time, I became sick with fever, the first time I had missed any duty, and was sent to the hospital in Richmond. Here I stayed for several weeks. On recovering I asked for a furlough, but on account of my age was discharged. I returned home and worked on my father's farm until later when I applied to the enrolling officer of Kershaw County for transportation, etc., to Company E., 2nd S. C. Volunteers. But to my surprise and regret he ordered me peremptorily to another command. . . .

Always I shall remember Sunday, April 28, 1861, when we set out for war, and the young men who on that bright spring day marched away so bravely. A majority of them found soldiers' graves. What a privilege it was to be associated with such men! And how rich the remembrance of them, their forms, faces, voices and characteristics! The years have rolled on, and I have won many friends—

> Yet my heart cannot part with its sorrow,
> When I think of the ones that are gone.

For a typical true story of a more mature soldier's experience we are indebted to Mrs. C. B. Robinson of Marion, Alabama, who sent the following reminiscences written by Captain W. H. May, including "incidents of fights and events during the war and some laughable occurrences during some of the battles, and accounts of some escapes of myself from the Yankees."

When war was declared I went to Norfolk, Virginia, with the 3rd Alabama Regiment and was elected first Lieutenant.

Was in the bombardment of Drewry's Bluff on James River where we repulsed the enemy.... Next engagement was Seven Pines, June 1. Fighting the day before had left the field horrible. We made a splendid charge but lost nearly half. Late in the evening I spread down my blanket with the mound of a newly made grave for my pillow, and tried to sleep, but for a long time there was no sleep. Added to the groans of wounded and dying men were the still more horrible groans of wounded and dying horses—something the war was to make all too familiar.

Next battle of note was Chancellorsville, where we lost Stonewall Jackson and the hope of the Confederacy.... It was the most terrible march we ever made, hot and dusty. As we reached the position from whence we made the famous charge, we were told in undertones to sit down and watch the road as a column of Yankee cavalry was coming. We were then on Hooker's right flank and he had taken the precaution to fell trees and cut the limbs to prevent attack and obstruct our passage. When we met these obstacles, their sharpshooters commenced firing on us.... It was a running fight from then on until nine at night. Now and then they would wheel cannon into position, but before they could fire more than two shots we would be upon them.

We never knew of General Jackson being wounded until late at night. As we were retiring, looking for a place to bivouac on the field, he was borne past us on a litter but no one knew it was he, *this being his order....*

While awaiting orders at Gettysburg I witnessed a most ludicrous affair between Tom Powell and a nest of yellow jackets. The latter was domiciled in rock about two feet square, and the bullets were flying fast and thick. The position was too desirable for Tom to abandon it to the little pests, and it became the most desperately contested point on our line between them and Tom. At times they would get so numerous that he would jump up, slapping, stamping and cursing, until he would hear and see the effect of the bullets, then down into the nest he would go again, and so on until he silenced them and held the position to the time we were ordered to charge....

Infantry soldiers often claimed that they took far greater risks than cavalry soldiers. In fact, early in the war General D. H. Hill is reported to have jeered, "I have never seen a dead soldier with spurs on!" His remark gives point to this humorous story told by Captain May:

Our corps, which had been sent to the Shenandoah Valley, was about 100 miles from Staunton, Virginia, from whence we had to walk.... In about twenty miles of our destination we had got into squads of from four to fifty, and I with three others met a wounded man who informed us he belonged to cavalry. I offered him $50 to go back to camp with me. It seemed to strike him with surprise and he wanted to know why I should offer such a proposition. On being told it was simply speculation—that I could easily get $100 to show a wounded cavalryman—I received the most elaborate cursing I ever got in my life!

I was put in command of the 3rd Alabama Regiment September 19, 1864. Before the command was turned over to me I had found a badly wounded color-bearer of the 26th Massachusetts Regiment. His leg was broken and wounded in three places. I had a breastworks of rails placed before him for protection from his own men who kept up a constant fire, both musketry and cannon. His name was John A. Brown, a nice man, and he told me he was a Mason. Wanted to make me a present of something, but had nothing but his Mason's pin. I told him my father was a Mason and not to let it trouble him, for what was done was for no purpose of reward.

Not every account of the war had the lighthearted touch of this veteran who could describe the horrors but at the same time see the humor that sometimes arose. The following story, for instance, told by Union General Lovell H. Rousseau after Shiloh, shows how doubly tragic death seems when it comes to the very young:

Two days after the battle I walked into the hospital tent on the ground where the fiercest contest had taken place. As I stepped into the tent and spoke to some one, I was addressed by a voice, the childish tone of which arrested my attention: "That's General Rousseau! General, I knew your son Dickey. Where is Dick? I knew him very well." Turning to him I saw stretched on the ground a handsome boy about sixteen years of age. The hectic glow and flush on the cheeks, his restless manner, and his gasping and catching his breath as he spoke, alarmed me. I knelt by his side and pressed his fevered brow with my hands, and would have taken the child into my arms if I could. "And who are you, my son?" said I. "Why, I am Eddy McFadden from Louisville," was the reply. "I know you, General, and I know your son Dick. I've played with him. Where is Dick?" I thought of my own dear boy, of what might have befallen him; that he, too, deluded by villains, might, like this poor boy, have been mortally wounded among strangers and left to die. My manhood gave way, and burning tears attested, in spite of me, my intense suffering. He was shot through the shoulder and lungs. I asked him what he needed. He said he was cold and the ground was hard. I sent him my saddle-blanket, and returned next morning with lemons for him and the rest. He died in a day or two. Peace to his ashes. I never think of this incident that I do not fill up as if he were my own child.

Mrs. Lillian Foley of Virginia economically describes the courage and determination of the Confederate soldier: "When my uncle was wounded in the neck in the Civil War, he quickly reached down, grabbed a handful of dirt, crammed it in the bullet hole to stop the blood, and kept on fighting." It amazes us today to read of wounded soldiers —even amputees—impatient to return to battle. No other fact illustrates so forcefully that the Civil War was a war whose cause the people themselves believed in. Most foreign wars are initiated by heads of government; many people fight them only because they must.

A few miles from the writer's old home when he was growing up lived a man who, together with his regiment, became a legend in his own lifetime. This man was Colonel John R. Lane who led the charge of the famous 26th North Carolina Infantry at Gettysburg after the beloved 21-year-old Colonel Harry K. Burgwyn was fatally wounded. It is conceded that this regiment had the heaviest loss in a single battle of any

Confederate regiment—and apparently the heaviest loss by any regiment on either side. On this point Facts About the Civil War *issued by the Civil War Centennial Commission says: "Some authorities accredit the 26th North Carolina Regiment with having incurred the greatest loss in a single battle recorded in the Civil War. At Gettysburg, it lost 708 of its men, or approximately 85 per cent of its total strength." The next highest losses in a single battle were incurred by the First Texas Regiment, C.S.A., at Antietam, and the First Minnesota Union Regiment, at Gettysburg, both 82 per cent. By comparison the casualties in the famous "Charge of the Light Brigade" at Balaklava were only 36 per cent.*

In a recent article on "Gallant Men of the Civil War" Bruce Catton begins by mentioning the 26th North Carolina and 24th Michigan Regiments at Gettysburg: "At the end of that fight each regiment had lost . . . four men out of five, most of them killed or wounded, since very few prisoners were taken from either regiment that day. . . . Braver soldiers than these could not be found in any war."

In all Civil War history we doubt that there is any more thrilling chapter than the story of the fourteen color-bearers in this fight. In those days it was still customary for each side to fly its flag in battle. Naturally the color-bearer was the primary target of the enemy, but in spite of the pre-eminent danger, soldiers were fanatically determined to keep the colors flying. During this first day of Gettysburg, the flag of the 26th North Carolina was shot down fourteen times as each bearer was killed or wounded. Colonel Burgwyn himself was waving the banner when mortally wounded, when the flag fell to the ground for the thirteenth time. Colonel Lane immediately assumed command and again raised the colors. Before the firing died away, he was shot in the jaw and mouth—and the flag fell for the fourteenth time that day.

Colonel Lane survived, but only 15 per cent of the regiment escaped death or serious wounds.

Apparently Texas pride and lack of humility were as evident and as affectionately tolerated in Civil War days as now. The Falling Flag contains this Texas story that sounds familiar to modern ears:

We moved up to the firing at a gallop, and as we passed along there came sweeping through the woods . . . a body of infantry in line, moving at a double quick upon the same point, which was but a short distance ahead of us. They were what was left of the famous "Texas Brigade." At this time the brigade counted about one hundred and thirty muskets, commanded by Colonel Duke. We had been fighting with them all summer, from Deep Bottom to New Market heights, to the lines around Richmond, and they recognized us as we rode along their front, and with a yell as fierce and keen as when their three regiments averaged a thousand strong, and nothing but victory had been around their flag, they shouted to us, "Forward boys, forward—*and tell them Texas is coming!*"

Of course not all Southern states embraced the cause of the Confederacy as exuberantly as did Texas. Maryland had many men enlisted in the armies of both sides, yet she did not secede. The too-little-known story behind her reasons for not seceding is told in these words from the Garrett County, Maryland, Historical Society records:

Maryland was considered to be a Southern state and it was believed she would follow Virginia out of the Union. The legislature was overwhelmingly for secession. Had Maryland seceded, the nation's capital would have been an island completely surrounded by seceded territory. The B. & O.

R.R., the National Road, and the Northwestern Turnpike would have been closed to the Union. President Lincoln took vigorous action to prevent secession. The leading members of the legislature were clapped into jail and kept there until it was assured there would be no secession.

And yet when the Confederates invaded Maryland many men and women reacted with as much hostility as Mrs. John Higgins of Rockville, Maryland, who wrote a letter to her mother June 29, 1863, in which she described the coming of the Rebs:

I got the children off to Sabbath school. As John came in the front gate on his return, I heard a terrific yell and saw six men on horseback rushing up to our gate and drawing up in line. Dora screamed "rebels, Ma!" I thought it impossible but the next moment I saw a whole column with the Rebel flag, charging furiously down past William Brewer's and the next moment heard a discharge of muskets and cannon.

I broke through the charging columns with the pistol balls flying and rushed through the back way to the church just in time to warn Mr. Higgins, Mr. Bowie, Mr. Dawson and Mr. Williams to stay in the vestry room for they were vowing vengeance on them.

There were three brigades of Rebels in all, about 8,000. They captured an incoming Federal wagon train of 170 wagons and swept the whole country of horses and servants. . . . During the day they [Rebels] brought in 600 prisoners, colored men, soldiers, and citizens and put them in the Court House. I thought verily they would tear the whole of the inside out of the Court House; their yells were so terrific on each fresh arrival of prisoners. . . .

Notwithstanding all, they behaved better than I expected.

Never entered the house. They had feasted off Uncle Abe's army rations. Had captured enough coffee, a *rarity*. They boasted they were *gentlemen and do not distress women and children and destroy dwellings.*

The sounds of battle were described in lusty detail by B. F. Taylor in his account of the battle of Chickamauga:

If anybody thinks that when men are stricken upon the field they fill the air with cries and groans, till it shivers with such evidence of agony, he greatly errs. An arm is shattered, a leg carried away, a bullet pierces the breast, and the soldier sinks down silently upon the ground, or creeps away if he can, without a murmur or complaint; falls as the sparrow falls, speechlessly; and like that sparrow, I earnestly believe, not without a Father. The horse gives out his fearful utterances of almost human suffering, but the mangled rider is dumb. The crash of musketry, the crack of rifles, the roar of guns, the shriek of shells, the Rebel whoop, the Federal cheer, and that indescribable undertone of rumbling, grinding, splintering sound, make up the voices of the battlefield.

Dr. William L. Daniel described the hideous aftermath of battle in a letter to his mother written on July 13, 1862, from Camp McLaws near Richmond, Virginia:

Bob arrived after all the fighting was over, but he saw the destruction of woods by cannon balls and smelt the horrible stench of the battlefield. To give you a little idea of what destruction is done: I went to a place where we took a Yankee battery and counted between fifty and sixty fine horses killed in a space of 200 yards square. These were the horses attached to the battery. I was detailed to help bury the dead, and such a task! I fell in with some Yankee surgeons and helped one cut off a wounded man's thigh, as he was scarce of help. Surgeons are not taken prisoners now, but are allowed to tend the wounded. I saw men—Yankees— lying in the field with legs mangled, arms broken, brains shot out, and alive on the third day after the fight. Oh! what suffering!

Did the soldiers—or most of them—come to regard death very differently from the way most of us in civilian life regard it? Can it be that they came to think of death, not as a malicious enemy to be fought, but as a not unfriendly instrument of fate—to be accepted as calmly as sunrise or sunset?

In reading great masses of material on the Civil War, you get the feeling, too, that soldiers then had an unfaltering faith in a life after death. The majority of them seemed to know that death was not the end, that they were going to something better when they died. This faith must have sustained and comforted them through many a bitter moment of pain and terror.

While unable to identify the author of the following report found among other old records of Civil War days, it seems to have all the earmarks of authenticity. A soldier who had served as a steward in a hospital several months said:

"I thought I had seen brave men in battle, but I never knew what bravery was till I went to the hospital. They often told me to fix them out."

"What is that?"

"Well, they would see that the doctor gave them up, and they would ask me about it. I would tell them the truth. I told one man that, and he asked how long? I said not over twenty minutes. He did not show any fear—they never do. He put up his hand so, and closed his eyes with his own fingers, and then stretched himself out, and crossed his arms over his breast. 'Now, fix me,' he said. I pinned the toes of his stockings together; that was the way we laid corpses out; and he died in a few minutes. His face looked as pleasant as if he was asleep, and smiling. Many's the time the boys have fixed themselves that way before they died."

CHAPTER TWO

The Reminiscences of
Berry Benson

MANY DIARIES WRITTEN DURING CIVIL WAR DAYS ARE CHARAC-
terized by a quaintness of expression that has the same charm
as an old-fashioned photograph album. In contrast Berry
Benson's Reminiscences, written fifteen years after the end
of the Civil War, tells its story in words no less charming
but which will sound entirely familiar to "Benson 1963"—to
whom he refers as the relative he hoped would one day read
his book.

Berry Greenwood Benson was born in Bamberg, South
Carolina, in 1843. Although his family later settled in Georgia
and Berry grew up there, he enlisted in the 1st Regiment of
South Carolina Volunteers, nineteen days after South Carolina seceded. He fought in many of the major battles of the
war: Fredericksburg, Manassas, Winchester, Chancellorsville,
Sharpsburg. Throughout the war he kept a diary in extraor-
dinary fullness from which he later wrote his Reminiscences.

After the war Berry taught school, worked as an account-
ant, and wrote, not too successfully, many poems and short
stories. He never lost his exuberant lust for life and adventure
or his consuming desire for new knowledge. At 65 he learned
to read French. At 75 he conducted a door-to-door canvass

in Augusta, Georgia, to find homes for 160 French orphans. He and his own family took care of five.

Berry Benson stands in striking contrast to some reluctant soldiers of our time. He was passionately partisan to the cause of the South, and when war came rushed to embrace it with every nerve alert to all the experiences and adventures it had to offer.

His was one of the most varied and thrilling autobiographies produced by any soldier, North or South. First he tells what a battle is—and is not—like.

Since I am writing this as an heirloom which I hope will go down amongst my descendants for a long time, and since there will be many who will go through life without ever experiencing the excitement of battle, and who, unless they have very different ideas of these things from what I had in my boyhood before I had seen for myself, may get quite false notions in regard to it, I want to try to tell something of how the fighting really goes on. I supposed a battle was carried on in the order and style of a first-class drill, knees all bent at the same angle and at the same moment, guns leveled on a line that was even as a floor, and every trigger pulled at one moment making a single report.

For a battlefield is not a drillroom, nor is battle an occasion for drill, and only the merest semblance of order is maintained. I say *semblance* of order, for there *is* an undercurrent of order in tried troops that surpasses that of the drillroom. It is that order that springs from the confidence comrades have in one another—from the knowledge that these messmates of yours, whether they stand or lie upon the ground, close together or scattered apart, in front of you three paces or in rear of you six, in the open or behind a tree or a rock—the confidence that these though they do not "touch elbows to the right," are nevertheless keeping dressed upon the colors in some rough fashion, and that the line will not move forward and leave them there, nor will they move back and leave the line.

A battle is entered into mostly in as good order and with as close a drill front as the nature of the ground will permit, but at the first "pop! pop!" of the rifles there comes a sudden loosening of the ranks, a freeing of selves from the impediment of contact, *and every man goes to fighting on his own hook; firing as, and when he likes, and reloading as fast as he fires.* He takes shelter wherever he can find it, so he does not get too far away from his company, and his officers will call his attention to this should he move too far. He may stand up, he may kneel down, he may lie down, it is all right—though mostly the men keep standing, except when silent under fire, then they lie down.

And it is not officers alone who give orders. The command to charge may come from a private in the line whose quick eye sees the opportunity, and whose order then brooks no delay. Springing forward, he shouts, "Charge, boys, charge!" The line catches his enthusiasm, answers with yells, and follows him in the charge. Generally it is a wild and spontaneous cry from many throats along the line, readily evoked by the least sign of wavering in the enemy.

A battle is too busy a time, and too absorbing, to admit of a good deal of talk. Still you will hear such remarks and questions as: "How many cartridges you got?" "My gun's getting mighty dirty." "What's become of Jones?" "Looky here, Butler, mind how you shoot; that ball didn't miss my head two inches." "Just keep cool, will you; I've got better sense than to shoot anybody." "Well, I don't like your standing so close behind me, nohow." "I say, look at Lieutenant Byson behind that tree." "Purty rough fight, ain't it Cap'n?" "Cap'n, don't you think we better move up a little, just along that knoll?" All this is mixed and mingled with fearful yells, and maybe curses too, at the enemy.

[Next Berry Benson describes the love of a soldier for his flag.]

And a charge looks just as disorderly. With a burst of yells, a long, wavering, loose-jointed line sweeps rapidly forward, only now and then one or two stopping to fire, while here and there drop the killed and the wounded; the slightly wounded, some of them giving no heed but rushing on, while others run hurriedly, half-bent to the rear. The colors drop, are seized again, again drop, and are again lifted, no man in reach daring to pass them by on the ground—colors not bright and whole and clean as when they came fresh from the white embroidering fingers, but since clutched in the storm of battle with grimy, bloody hands, and torn into shreds by shot and shell.

Oh, how it thrilled the heart of a soldier, when he had been long away from the army, to again catch sight of his red battle flag, upheld on its white staff of pine, its tatters snapping in the wind! "A red rag," there be those who will say, "a red rag, tied to a stick, and that is all!" And yet—that red rag, crossed with blue, with white stars sprinkling the cross within, tied to a slim, barked-pine sapling, with leather thongs cut from a soldier's shoe, this rough, red rag my soul loved with a lover's love. How often in long prison days have I sat and dreamed over it, imagining friends come to release us, and my first meeting with its fairness! How I clasped it in my arms, and kissed it, and cried over it! As I might do today, alas, forgetful of restraint, could I once more see the old flag floating in the wind!

[On the night before battle strong men turned for comfort to their Bibles.]

. . . The night before the battle, not knowing that we would not be engaged next day; indeed, taking it for granted we

would be, there were many little private talks around the
fires, friends giving instructions to do so and so in case of
being killed, to write to such and such a one, and say....
Sergeant Mackey gave a number of messages to the men to
talk to his people at home, saying he felt that he was to be
killed next day. On the eve of all our battles there was of
course more or less of this forethought and preparation for
death, but I remember it particularly of this one. Due, it
may be, to the strain of my own thoughts at the time;—just
as probably like action on my part on the eve of the battle
of Chancellorsville causes me to remember especially vividly
the number of men I then saw looking into their Bibles,
picking out here and there favorite texts for comfort and
encouragement. And it was with no degree whatever of
shamefacedness that the men at such solemn times turned
to their Testaments; and the Book would, not unlikely, be
passed from one to another. And such men were foremost in
the charge and rearmost in retreat. It was Hawthorne of
the Sharpshooters who fell at Petersburg, far in advance of
the line, shouting, "The Lord is my shield and buckler!"

... At a little place called Harrisonville [probably Jeffer-
sonton] we had the heartiest laugh. The turnpike we were
traveling had been passed over back and forth already during the war, by first one army and then the other; and
altho' we were constantly greeted with the cries: "Hurrah
for South Carolina! Hurrah for Georgia!" or whatever might
be the state from which came the troops then passing, there
was with us a faint doubt whether the enemy when they
passed through might not receive from some of the people
the same kind of greeting. Not from inclination, we knew
well enough, but to keep on the good side of the powers
that be.

Well, as we passed a house where some ladies were standing, they asked as the head of the regiment came up: "What

Regiment is this?" "First South Carolina." "Hurrah for South Carolina—hurrah for South Carolina!" came the sweet voices of the dear women, chorused at the close by the piping voice of a little fellow not much more than a baby—"Hurrah for Sout Caliny Massachute!" "Hush, hush, hush!" from the women—but the cat was out of the bag, and such a laugh as the boys set up! "Hurrah for Sout Caliny Massachute!" was a standing joke for a long time. But it was only thought of as a good joke, for the people everywhere were eminently and truly patriotic, and they were exceedingly generous, and the women seemed to us very angels out of the sky.

[Benson describes the merciless heckling soldiers gave seemingly able-bodied men who were not in uniform.]

... It was somewhere about Salem, I think, that two young women ran out from the house on our approach, and stood at the gate, with eyes filled with tears, blessing us, and telling us we were the first Confederate soldiers they had yet seen. They had seen their enemy's soldiers in plenty but never their own before. Sometimes as we passed one of those large Virginia mansions, or going through a village, we would find a group of ladies standing at the side of the road with buckets of milk, or water, or maybe biscuits and ham or butter, or cold chicken, which they would give over into the hands that would be thrust out to receive as the column of half-famished men swept forward. Gratitude for such kindnesses we all felt, of course, but gratitude had little power to check the spirit of fun that lay in us. Certainly a citizen man was sure of a galling fire of banter if he showed himself in tongue-reach. It was a steady flow of, "Does your mother know you're out?" "Come out of that hat; I know you're there, I see your legs." "Lie down melish', I'm agwine to pop a cap!" Or, perhaps, accompanied by an unblushing stare, a "Hoo-hoo! Hoo-hoo!" (hooting cry in imitation of an owl) "*Who*-are-you?" (heavy stress on the "Who"). It is impossible to put on paper the rendering of that cry, but performed by an artist, it out-hooted the owl, and was simply irresistible. Nothing could have stood it but "an iron dog." When a halt was made to sleep, all the houses in the neighborhood would be besieged by soldiers, buying or begging something to eat. The earliest comers fared the best, or they got the cooked provisions, while latecomers must be content with flour, meal and raw meat, which they must cook themselves as best they could. Some of the men begged without any lack of cheek; one standard tale was of a fellow who appeals to the lady of the house: "Please, ma'am, give me a drink of water I'm so hungry I ain't got no place to sleep"—all in one breath.

[Berry Benson's next notes concern crude methods of cooking—and "the proudest look I ever saw on mortal man."]

... Having pursued the enemy as far as we could [in Virginia], we were brought to a halt. We camped in a piece of woods, and rations were issued, meat and flour. If I remember rightly these were the first rations that had been issued to us since we began to march. We had been living on the spoils from the enemy. But now not a cooking utensil of any kind could be had, high or low. The meat could be broiled on the coals, but how to cook flour without oven, frying pan or something, how even to make it into dough? Some heated stones after mixing the dough in dirty handkerchiefs; some baked in the ashes.

I cast about and found an old broken ploughshare in a field on which we baked. But the neatest device of all and one which at that early day created much interest and amusement, was the making of the dough into a long rope, which was then wrapped spirally round a ramrod, the ramrod being laid horizontally before the fire on two small wooden forks set in the ground. By turning the ramrod, all parts of the dough were by turns exposed to the fire and so baked, being broken off in pieces when done. (It then miraculously disappeared.) It was on one of these days, about the close of the fighting, while our line was standing on the edge of the road, that I recognized old John Seitz of Morris Island memory, who was marching past in a column of troops going by. I hailed him, he turned, hailed me in reply, and with a parting salute, he went on, and I have never seen him since. It was thus, in the midst of the hurry and confusion of battle and moving into position, that friends often met perhaps only to wave the hand or the cap; or at best but to stop for a moment, shake hands and say: "Goodbye, God bless you, old fellow," and on again, lost amidst the multitude.

Have you ever seen a proud man? One who looked proud? I have seen the personification of pride; a man bearing in his face the proudest look I ever saw in mortal man. And he was barefoot. It was in the Valley, after the battle of Sharpsburg, as we were marching along the turnpike, a newfallen snow on the ground, that, happening to cast my eyes to one side, I saw him, a young man, tall and vigorous, but utterly barefoot in the snow, standing in a fence corner, his gun leaning against his shoulder—and of all proud faces I have ever seen, his was the proudest. It was a pride that seemed to scorn not only the privation and cold, but the exposure of his sufferings to other eyes, and even the very pity that it called forth. . . .

[Benson reports an exploit so daring that even the enemy cheered the hero.]

My partner, Mat Hitt, tells [this story]. . . . In Maryland, two lines of battle fronted each other, partly seen, partly hidden; and the Confederate commander, to get a clearer idea of the force opposing him, called for a volunteer to undertake the dangerous duty of riding down the enemy's front near enough to count the flags as he went. Mat Hitt rode out from the ranks, and received his orders. Mounted on a splendid animal, but with a uniform which consisted of a red flannel shirt, a pair of white cotton drawers (being trouserless), and a broad felt hat with its brim pinned up in front with a horseshoe nail, he rode straight to the front very deliberately, the enemy watching him without firing, not understanding the movement. But getting within close range, near enough for his purpose, he suddenly wheeled his horse, spurring down their line at a furious gallop, *wildly cheered by the enemy the whole way,* and not being fired upon once! That was gallantry on both sides!

[A dream of what the war will seem like when it is long, long past:]

... One night of this march, while we were yet in the Valley, will forever remain impressed upon my memory, not for aught of circumstance in the time itself, but by reason of the train of thought into which I fell.

Night had already come, the roads were exceedingly rough, there had been so much rain we often went over shoe in the mud, and we were every minute expecting to turn off from the road into the woods to camp. Still we marched on, till tired, hungry and wet, we longed to halt. Then here and there began to spring up lights in the woods, the fires of other troops now going into camp, so we knew we would stop soon. I fell into a reverie. I said to myself, Berry Benson, do you see those fires? They are the campfires of soldiers, real living soldiers who have just come out of battle. Yes, I said, and I am one of them. Forward I look and there moves the long dark line of men, four abreast, each with his gun aslant on his shoulder; behind it is the same. There! another light—I see it spring up in the darkness. I see dark moving forms about it. I look and feel it all to be the living present. But, Berry Benson, that fire you now behold (see how red it gleams!)—that fire will die down, days will go by, years will go by, and you will remember it, but it will be a thing of the long past (see how red it gleams!), and you will be otherwhere, if you go safe through the war, at peace, at home, going about your daily business (hark to the tramp of the army!), and the fire will be gone, and the tramp of men will be gone, the road will be empty and silent (how red the fire gleams!), and all, all will be but a picture, a memory of long ago—oh! sweet to remember!—I feel the pain on my shoulder, it is the press of the strap of my cartridge box—stop! is it real? is it no dream, but something that *is*, and is now, when tomorrow has not yet come, nor the next day, nor the year gone by, nor the war ended. And are these lights and this dark column, with its tramp through the slush, and its shouts and its laughter (hark to the voices!)—are these not memories only that I, far off, the war long over, am calling up of a time that was? No, no, see how the fire gleams! list to the tramp and the voices! the shouts and the laughter! these *are*, and *are*, and *are*.

And yet look good, Berry Benson, drink in the night and the time that now *is* and lives, the very *now*, for soon, soon it will be drifted back in the past, a time to remember. Take your fill of joy of it, for it is a time of war that, bitter as it now is, through hunger and cold and fatigue and drowsiness, will yet ere long be sweet to remember for its color and life and passion, in days that by its side will be dull and tame and spiritless. Cold lie the ashes of camps in the Valley; untrodden are its ways of soldiers' feet; the springs are no more merry with the jingling of canteens; not any more do the dry leaves rustle under foot as the line files off in the woods for its night's bivouac!

[The friendliness of Northern and Southern pickets often mentioned by other writers is here again reported.]

... We picketed the Rappahannock at Moss Neck Church, one's turn to picket coming every few days, 24 hours being the term. We became quite friendly with the enemy's pickets posted on the opposite side and could talk with them, and exchange newspapers. The exchange was made by taking a piece of board or bark, fixing a stick upright on it as a mast, with the paper attached to this as I said. By setting the sail properly, the wind would carry it across, from one side to the other, as it was wanted to go. Once a Federal band came down to the river and played "Dixie." We cheered this vociferously, of course. Then it played "Yankee Doodle," and the enemy cheered. Then "Home, Sweet Home," and the cheer went up loud and long from both sides of the river. One day, on picket at an old barn, where there were a good many rats, some of the boys in jest proposed to catch some and see how they would eat, broiled. But the jest was changed to earnest, and soon some were killed and on the coals, and given a trial, B. K. [Berry's brother] being one of the ringleaders. They gave it as their opinion that rat tasted like young squirrel, and the rest of us took their word for it. If it were the time back, though, I don't think I should be squeamish. I overcame prejudice against the bull frog and found him very nice. On the margin of the river grew great beds of calamus which some of the boys were fond of chewing; I didn't like it. But if some 1963 Benson ever pickets along the Rappahannock, let him taste the calamus, which will still be there.

[To Benson, "Stonewall" was "the valiantest soldier of the land," and his death accordingly lamented.]

... Stopping to rest in the woods, we stacked arms just on the side of the road and lay down. While lying here, we heard a faint yell in the distance, back on the road, and the men began to say: "Jackson—or a rabbit; Jackson—or a rabbit." But the yell continuing and growing louder and nearer, everybody says: "It's Jackson—it *is* Jackson!" And directly came the sound of horses' feet galloping as all then rose, waving hats in the air and cheering the rider. Then came Jackson at a furious gallop, looking neither to the right nor the left—not even paying the least heed to a stand of arms belonging to my company that stood in the road, but riding over them scattering them right and left as though they had been broom sticks only. And after him, some fifty yards behind, his aide, trying to keep him in sight. I have often thought that of all relics of the war, I would rather have the gun that his horse's hoof struck just then. For the mark must yet be plain upon it, wherever it is—and where it may now be, who can tell? For doubtless its owner prized it but little, and parted with it easily—strange that may seem, yet see, however dearly I might buy it now, the thought of securing it then never came to me. Probably I would have swapped my own rifle for it without good boot. Maybe I would have considered the bruise a *defect*.

"Jackson—or a rabbit!" That was the cry always made when a distant yell was heard, for whether one or the other, no pair of eyes would ever rest on him but the mouth under them opened and gave vent to a prolonged yell. They were both cheered the same—only Jackson with "hats off."

The other time I speak of was at Harper's Ferry just after its surrender. We were all occupied in one thing or another, the prisoners moving about freely amongst us, though well guarded, when the cry was heard, and the clattering hoofs. "What's the matter?" asked the prisoners. "Jackson's coming!" was the answer as all feet rushed to the road, and such a cheer as was set up by men in gray and men in blue, has seldom been heard! For the prisoners, all, cheered him just as lustily and as heartily as we did ourselves. And we felt very kindly toward them for it.

And now Jackson lay mortally wounded, his brilliant story drawing to a close. And as I lay in my cot in Manchester, I heard the bells of Richmond tolling his death. Such gloom therefore, as fell upon all the people! For the valiantest soldier of the land lay dead, and there was none other like him.

[A clean white shirt made Benson suspect at Fredericksburg.]

...I remember very well on going through the camps, before reaching my own, being hailed with continuous cries of "Hospital Rat! Hospital Rat!" About hospitals, just as they do about hotels and such places, rats always collected in numbers, big ones, and got fat off stealings and waste, of course, and as there were some men who shirked the camp and the campaign, and, under pretense of being sick, spent a large portion of their time at hospitals, the good soldiers conceived a natural hearty dislike and contempt for these, and applied to them the epithet of Hospital Rat, as implying their having made the hospital a permanent abode. But as soldiers are not very discriminating in their judgments, or rather, because the temptation to fling a stone is too enticing, they seldom stopped to inquire whether the passerby really deserved the name or not; the wearing of clean clothes without holes in them was evidence which, although it might be merely circumstantial, was to them strong enough to warrant the attack. Private or officer, he could not escape the shelling, and many's the man who, having arrived close to his camp early in the evening, has hung around in the woods till dusk, before venturing to run the gantlet. "Hospital Rat! Hospital Rat." The stereotyped reply to which was, by those courageous enough to face it: "You go to hell!" which only thickened the abuse. I remember walking once through a strange camp at Fredericksburg, having on a clean white shirt, albeit of coarse cotton, bosom and all, but its whiteness made it a target, and I was hailed with, "clean shirt! clean shirt! come out of that shirt!" The face of the aforesaid "iron dog" would grow red under such a volley.

[Soldiers cheering made an impression never to be forgotten.]

... Hardly ever, until reaching Spotsylvania Courthouse, were we in fields, always the Wilderness. While waiting stationary, behind the breastworks, not knowing when the enemy might attack, all at once we heard cheering far on the right, so far that it was almost inaudible through faintness. But gradually it grew louder and louder, nearer, nearer, until we knew it was a cheer which, starting on the right of the army, was passing down to the left, taken up in succession by the troops as it approached. Nearer, nearer, and now it is just on our right hand, and we take it up, and as we quiet we hear it passing on, on, to the left, gradually dying out in the distance. But it has hardly passed us, when we hear another cheer coming from the right, and it slips down and down, till we take that up in turn, only to hear a third on its way, which also we sent on its way, and so on till ten cheers had passed like waves the length of the army. I think there were generally three cheers in motion on the line at one time; when the extreme right heard one dying out they would start another.

This kind of cheering I never heard before, but I have often since. ... No one who has never heard it can appreciate its splendid effect. It is grand. Hearing it at first faintly, in the far distance, it comes like the breath of a wind, drawing nearer and nearer, till it reaches you with the blast as of trumpets, then fading away again in the distance—one must be a soldier to feel its full charm. Since then I have often heard this extended cheering, but never so well executed nor with such sublime effect as that night in the Wilderness. After the ten cheers had all passed, came then a message started and forwarded in the same way, but we could not distinguish the words till close to us; then we heard: "Grant's wounded! Grant's wounded!" and so we passed it, but just to our left they got it wrong and (passing down only the last syllable) the message went on its way: "Grant's dead! Grant's dead!" So the right of the army had it that Grant was wounded, the left that he was dead. . . .

This mode of transmitting messages was often used to good purpose. For instance, the message might be conveyed a mile or two very rapidly, "Tell Major———General——— wants to see him at once at the Dabney House." . . . Messages were carried very quickly this way, and without trouble.

[We now come to Benson's description of the bloodiest of all his battles—Spotsylvania.]

. . . How describe this terrible battle—the bloodiest, the hardest fought, the most obstinate of the war, for the ground covered? . . . The flags crowded together. The firing was incessant, only lulls of short duration, when both sides would go to shouting to each other, urging surrender. But neither would consider the idea, and again the battle would begin.

Once a small party of Confeds, being subjected to a fierce crossfire, raised a white flag. Immediately the cry arose, "Shoot them fellows! Shoot them fellows!" and it was jerked down. But the enemy seeing the flag, ceased firing and also raised a white flag as a sign of truce. An officer came forward saying the surrender would be accepted. But he was told that it was no surrender, that the white flag (a handkerchief) had been raised without authority.

There was no artillery. There may have been a little in the beginning, but there was none now. Artillery could not live in such a close, hand-to-hand fight. It was crowded out. Branches of trees were falling, shot off by rifle balls! A tree twenty inches in diameter fell, cut down by rifle balls! The stump of it is now in Washington in the National Museum. . . . Where the lines overlapped, the men said they and the enemy both mostly fired without showing their heads above the work, which was certain death. Guns were loaded, held up to the breastwork, depressed, and the trigger pulled with the thumb. One man, I think it was Owens of Company H, told me he several times took in his hand the barrel of a gun pointing down on him, held it up till it was fired and then let it go. Only there were some men who *would* stand up. Stand up, calling for loaded guns which were passed to them, they would fire a few shots and fall, shot through the head. It was Owens with two or three others, who at one time occupied a small detached mound. "Cannon-pit," Owens called it, . . . which being a little elevated gave a better command of the field. They had a whole box of ammunition. From this point they kept up a continuous fire. By some means they took a prisoner. Him they compelled to load guns, or pass cartridges, I forget now which Owens said. That was wrong.

Just when it was that I, lying down behind the breastwork, worn and tired, without food for so long, and without sleep since two nights before, fell asleep, while still the bullets came hurtling down the breastwork, I don't know; but fall asleep I did, and I suppose I was taken for dead, for nobody waked me. Some time in the night, though, I was awakened by the tramp of a large body of men rushing by. I jumped up and asked: "What troops are these?" "Louisiana Battalion." A dead man lay by my side. The firing now, if not altogether ceased (I think it had not) was much weaker, and I soon learned that the Confederate line was under order to retire from the position, a few at a time, and take up a position at an inner line of works which, I believe, had been built through the day. This was done, and the position abandoned. Going out in the dark, I fell into a ditch, an entrenchment, I suppose, and came with my whole weight on somebody who gave a fearful groan, but whether he was a wounded man or not, I don't know.

This description can give but the faintest idea of that

terrible battle of Spotsylvania, "Bloody Angle" or Horse Shoe Bend as it is also called. About daylight the regiment began to gather together, the different groups of them, and organize as well as possible. Everybody seemed fagged out. . . .

[Benson's story next turns to a most daring and dangerous mission and the part played by quick wit and a strangely intuitive ingenuity.]

. . . On the evening of 16 May the brigade took position on the breastwork. A picket being put out, the S.S. [Sharpshooters] were allowed to sleep. Some small pines had been felled and the boughs piled, and on these we spread our blankets, the ground being wet. I had fallen asleep, but was waked by hearing some person talking. I listened and heard Captain Dunlap ask for one or two persons to go scouting.

I rose and offered my services. "You are just the man I want," he said. "Take three men and report to Captain Langdon Raskell, at Brigade Headquarters." I told him two would do, and Wesley Norton of Company A and Russell of Company——volunteering, I took them. Captain H. said that General Lee suspected the enemy of moving, or being about to move, by the Telegraph Road from Fredericksburg to Richmond, and he therefore ordered every brigade commander to learn what the enemy were doing in his immediate front.

I asked whether I should go out to the front or go around and get in their rear. He said I might do as I chose. I preferred going round and fixed an hour to return next day, upon which he replied that I must be back within two hours. I answered that it was impossible then to get to the rear, as we were now somewhere near the center of the army. And I doubted my ability to learn anything of consequence in front. "Then if you can't get the information *outside*, you must go *inside*," he said.

This was a stunner. To get amongst the enemy by striking

their flank might be practicable, but to penetrate their lines directly in front, and escape observation, would be almost impossible. But I quickly made up my mind what to do. I asked the time. "Eleven o'clock."

With my two men I passed out to our picket line and found the first group *asleep!* Just think! When only four days before we had such a terrible lesson in the surprise of Johnson's men, at dawn, at the Horse Shoe Bend! That cost such a battle, too. We roused the men, and asked for their officer. He was called; when he came, I gave him a rasping lecture, to all which he replied deferentially: "Yes, Colonel, it was very wrong in the men; they were very tired; but I'll see that it don't happen again, Colonel," etc., etc. We all three enjoyed the "Colonel" part of the apology, hugely, [Berry was a sergeant] but I really felt very much vexed at their intense carelessness.

My plan now was to draw as near as possible to the enemy's picket line and listen for the sound of troops moving, which if we could hear we would report; if we should hear nothing, to leave my two men outside, while I made an effort to penetrate the lines undiscovered; should I be discovered, then to claim to be a Federal scout, trusting to the chance of their letting me go into camp without further questions,— an exceedingly slim chance, I know, but I knew there were fools in the army as well as elsewhere.

Should I fail in this chance (and I expected failure), then I would, after having gained all possible information with eyes and ears, endeavor to effect my escape. My purpose was to make a straight run from camp for the picket line. I believed I could run through without being stopped; and as for the shooting that would follow my passing out of the picket line, I wasn't much afraid of that in the night.

I knew the ground pretty well, for I had been sharpshooting over it for a week; so, instructing my two men to keep fifty yards behind me, and whenever they heard me halted or talking to anybody, to wait a while, and if I did not return, to report the fact, I proceeded toward the enemy's picket line.

I had got pretty close, and was hoping that amongst the pine bushes I might get in unnoticed, when, having a wet place to cross, my foot made a slight noise. "Who comes there?" cried a sentinel. "A friend," I answered. "Come in, then," was the reply. Had I up to this time heard any sounds that I could have reported to Captain Haskell as of troops moving, I should have turned and gone back, but I had heard nothing, so it only remained to me, in obedience of orders, to essay my other plan. I walked quietly up to the pickets, whom I saw to be in strong force along a low breastwork, and came among them. "What are you doing out there?" "I've been scouting down the rebel lines." "Where did you get out?" "Lower down on the left; I belong to Hancock's Corps." (I knew that corps was there.) Then followed questions as to division, brigade, and regiment. These I answered satisfactorily, having before this posted myself from prisoners, so I was not afraid of making the mistake of locating a regiment in a wrong brigade, etc. I am not sure but I even named the officers. I went on to say that having been scouting along the rebel lines I intended making a short cut back through the camps, instead of going the roundabout way I had come. "Well, it may be all right," said the officer, "but I'll have to send you up to Brigade Headquarters." "All right," I answered carelessly. He detailed two men to go with me, letting me carry my gun for myself. On the way I kept listening for sounds of marching troops, but everything was still. So I must further defer escape, and face the Brigadier, where I feared trouble. And if my instructions had not been so positive to "come back with information," I think I should then have made a run back for the picket line. Passing through a good deal of camp, my guards stopped me at the door of a large tent and announced to the occupant that they had a man in custody who claimed to be a Federal scout. He was lying down in his tent, with no light burning. "What regiment do you belong to?" "——New York." "You are a Southern soldier!" "You are altogether mistaken, sir." "You are a Southern soldier. What state are you from?" "New York." "You are a Southern soldier." "What makes you think I am a Southern soldier?" "I know it by your voice." "Well, sir, you were never more mistaken in anything in your life; you may keep me till morning, and send me then under guard to General Hancock, if you wish; then you will know." I made this bold speech as really the safest thing I could do. I was obliged to maintain my original position; and I feared that an obstinate maintenance of it would cause him to give me a personal inspection which would undo me, being clad in gray, and I thought that, being sleepy, he might say to the guard, keep him till morning, and I'll send him to General Hancock. Then I would have till daylight to escape. But his reply to my proposition was immediate and decisive. I heard him move; a match was struck; a candle lit. "Come in here!" It was all up. I threw back the flap of the tent and stepped inside, rifle and all. "Aha!" he said, as he cast his eyes on me, "What state are you from?" "South Carolina!" "Aha!" then he broke out in a laugh, and I followed suit. He was a mighty clever fellow. Sweitzer his name was, he told me, *Colonel* Sweitzer, commanding a brigade. Told me he had lived a while in the South, and recognized my voice as Southern, the first word I spoke. He talked right pleasantly with me for some time, asked me a good many general questions (nothing that I would not willingly answer), amongst other things how our army fared for food. Now, it happened that when I knew I was going out to scout I thought I might want something to eat before I got back, so I went to Company H and got a fresh baked loaf of bread from "Promptly" [the cook], instructing him to take my rations when they came next morning, in payment. And this was a very nice loaf, better bread than his hard tack, I knew, so I handed it to him and asked him to try it, saying we got plenty of that. (Everything being fair in war, I hope that was pardonable.) He broke off a piece and ate it, and said it was excellent. Then, after a little more light, cheerful talk, he bade me good-night and wished me a speedy exchange, for which I thanked him, intending to exchange myself before daylight, if possible. Before leaving, he ordered the guard to take my gun. . . . As the guard conducted me through the camp I continued on the alert for signs or sounds of movement, but I neither saw nor heard anything. Arrived at a little cluster of tents, my guards delivered me to another guard, asking of the sergeant in whose care I was left a certificate that I had been delivered to him. This he gave, writing with a pencil, by the light of a candle. I was now conducted a little farther, to the edge of a little pine thicket, beyond which I saw heavier woods. Here were half a dozen or so, perhaps ten to twelve, flytents stretched, with men in them sleeping. Outside was a low fire by which sat a guard, rifle in hand. To him I was delivered.

[Another desperate gamble almost paid off for Berry in his next activity.]

In an instant, I conceived my plan of operations. It was to pump this guard as to the movements of troops if I could, get him to tell me all he knew, and then make a run for the big woods, and trust to fortune for the rest. Not wishing to appear to be pumping him, I thought the best way to draw him out would be to go to bragging for my own side, this would set him to bragging for his, and I hoped he would let some cats out of his bag while doing it. It worked to a charm. He told me a good deal I wanted to hear. Only I remember

he told me of a movement of the Corcoran Legion, and of
the heavy artillery men who had been manning the defenses
of Washington being brought to the front, giving numbers,
and more. This I stored up.

And now a thought struck me. I knew that our men often
kept guard, in camp this way, with unloaded guns, and if
I could only satisfy myself that his was unloaded, then I
could make the bolt with greater confidence. But how to
find this out? Well, there was a way. Leaning against a little pine just at my left hand was a rifle, belonging to another of the guards, and I said to myself, "They are all apt
to be alike, all loaded or all unloaded, let's try this one." So
I went on bragging and directly said: "Why, we can beat
you drilling, even that's been proved. Now, in the manual
of arms I don't pretend to be one of the best, but I daresay
I can go through it better than you." And with these words
I picked up the gun—he looking at me and saying little. I
carried the gun to a "shoulder," to the "order," back to the
"shoulder," to the "present," back to the "shoulder," briskly
obeying the commands as I gave them to myself in a low
voice; then I gave the order "Load in nine times! Load!"
The gun passed to my left side, the butt dropped to the
ground; my right hand went back as though to the cartridge
box; I bit the end off the imaginary cartridge; placed it in the
muzzle; drew the ramrod; passed it down the barrel; (the
gun was empty!) replaced the ramrod; brought the gun to
the right side; cocked it; drew a cap out of my vest pocket
for cap box, and capped the gun—I mean I actually put a
cap on the gun. "There! can you beat that?" I asked. And
I just had it on my tongue to say: "Goodbye, old fellow!"
when the corporal of the guard came from somewhere, and
posted another man in the old guard's place, who retired.

So I waited, preferring to run from one than from two.
The corporal, a tall, well-made fellow, leaned his gun against

the tree right by the side of the gun I had had, and stood by the fire a minute or two, then picking up his gun, he told me to come with him. We went out, he in front, along a line of wagons parked, the horses eating. Just beyond the wagons, ten yards or so on my right lay the edge of an oak wood, and I saw no tents in it. As I said, the corporal was in front of me, about a step, but also a little to my left, as he walked. His rifle was thrown over his right shoulder. I thought one big, jumping thought of my sweetheart, and my left hand fell heavily on the gun barrel, which, as I turned and sprang amongst the horses, I heard ring on the ground. "Halt! Halt!" rang the corporal's voice, to which I paid no heed as I sped.... I ran down the hill then, in the open, as I never ran before ... the corporal still in pursuit, shouting, "Stop that man!" I gained the wood, almost broken down, but still determined to get into the depth of the wood before slacking speed, when oh, disaster!—sharp upon my left came a party of armed men running who caught me and held me fast.

[At this point Benson's luck ran out, and we next find him a prisoner of the enemy.]

The corporal came up and took charge of me, the whole party accompanying back to where they had me before....

I now realized the perilous position I was in. Having represented myself to the pickets as a Union scout; having persisted in this assertion when brought before the commanding officer; having gathered a certain amount of information from the guard; and then having attempted to get away with it—I did not need to overhear (as I did) such talk as "the d——d spy." I am free to confess I felt a good deal alarmed, the more so as all avenues of present escape being closed, my thoughts were all now diverted inward, and I was continually picturing to myself the possibilities of the morrow, in which a rope with a noose hanging from a tree was not the least conspicuous. When they first tied my hands behind my back and tied me to the tree, I thought of how the Indians tied up captives and then burnt them; now I thought of a drumhead court martial, of being tried and found guilty as a spy, of being hung in the woods and left there.... At length the compression of the ropes on my wrists became so painful (for they were tied very tight) that I asked if they would be so good as to change my position some way. The rest paid no heed, but one came forward, a sergeant, and untying the ropes, tied me again, with my hands over my head, to a low limb.... My pockets were searched and my pocket book, as it contained only a little Confed. money and stamps, but the diary was kept. When day came (Tuesday, May 17, 1864) I was untied and taken to the Headquarters of General Patrick, Provost Marshal. Thence I was taken to General Meade's headquarters. [To Berry's relief he was not tried for being a spy but was taken to Point Lookout Prison on Chesapeake Bay on May 23, 1864.]

... In the afternoon of Monday, May 23, 1864, about 500 prisoners were put aboard a steamer and carried down to Point Lookout Prison, where we arrived about 4 P.M. There we were drawn up in ranks sixteen deep, and answered to our names. The prison was a square or oblong enclosure of about ten acres, and was said to contain at that time about 10,000 prisoners. The prisoners were allowed to go in and out of the gates, at pleasure, all day; at sundown the gates were locked.

[Immediately after his arrival in prison Berry began to plan his escape. Since he saw at once that the easiest way would be by water, he spent every spare minute practicing swimming. He noticed with special interest the privies which were built out over the waters of the Chesapeake Bay—outside the prison walls. Benson's plans for escape from prison and how they were executed are told in the paragraphs which follow.]

In the afternoon [May 25, 1864), just before sundown, I was sitting on the beach waiting for the sergeant to come round and close the gates, when I was surprised to see the white guards around the prison being relieved by blacks. This was a matter of surprise, as the new guard always went on early in the morning. And the sergeant did not come to close the gates as usual, and it was now almost sundown. By sunset almost all the prisoners had gone in to their quarters. It began to grow dusk, and no sergeant yet coming, my heart began to beat faster. I would not lose a moment. It was yet too light, but a little later—I walked quickly into the camp, to my tent, hearing many, as I passed, talking about the gates being still opened. Unperceived by the guards, the whole prison was in a low fever of excitement. I put on my jacket and stockings. I put my hat in my bosom, under my shirt. My shoes, being thicksoled and heavy, I was afraid to take, as I expected to have a good deal of swimming. I took them, with my vest, and a few other articles, to Russell's tent, leaving a request with a tentmate that he would take care of them till I called for them. Then I went to the middle gate and stood in it awhile, waiting for it to grow a little darker. Now and then some one passed me going in and out. One said to me: "You'd better go away from here; some of these niggers'll shoot you." A party of six passed out, and went into the box [privy]. Directly they came back, but just as they got to the lower end of the plankway, I saw one of them, behind the others, squat and dart under it. The rest re-entered the prison. I had seen a man get under there a little while before. I now walked out, passing over the two men. In the box I turned round and saw four Negro sentinels standing over the gate. Nobody was in the box but me. Reaching down I caught hold of one of the wooden pillars and slid down into the water. It was breast deep. Backing slowly in the water that I might see to keep the box between me and the sentinels, I went into deeper and deeper water. When the water was up to my chin I turned and began to wade up the bay. The darkness had increased so much and I had got so far from shore, perhaps thirty or forty yards, that I thought my head would not be seen above the water. I passed the upper end of the prison; I passed the guards' quarters, the water all the time up to my neck. Then I ventured to come more in towards shore, but still keeping the water first breast deep, and after a while waistdeep. I was now a good way past the prison. The walking for my bare feet was easy, being fine smooth sand, or clay. Suddenly a sharp pain struck me in my feet,—I was no longer on sand or clay, but stumbling forward over raccoon oyster beds, and the shells were cutting my feet like knives! It could not have been worse walking over a bed of broken bottles. I struggled on and passed over the oysters, glad to get my wounded feet again on the sand. But again I struck the oyster beds, but set my lips and passed over. As I passed I reached down and broke off two or three with my hands. These I ate; biting the thin edges of the shells with my teeth so I could pull them apart with my fingers, to get the meat. I now approached nearer the shore, and came in to where the water was knee deep. But I found that my legs in passing one another splashed the surface, so I went out again to hip deep. This was the best depth. Behind me trailed a phosphorescent cloud of light in the water; there was even so much light made by the motion of my legs that I could see as low as my knees. I could see little fishes too that came playing around me, each in his own circle of light. I looked behind me. Far away lay the white walls of the prison. Out at sea were the lights of one or two passing ships. The moon had risen, but was veiled by broken heavy clouds; only now and then could I catch a gleam of it thro' their misty edges.

How happy I was! Despite my wounded feet, how happy I was! For I was free. I was escaped from those four, awful white walls, and with care and labor I would soon be under the red flag again.... I stood so and rested... *two miles* (probably not nearly so far) or nearly from Point Lookout Prison breathing the cool fresh free air of Maryland, no bayonets, nor walls, nor obedience,—only me and the fields and the woods wide and unbounded, and the sea and the sky and the wind and liberty. How my heart swelled! If I ever get to heaven will I feel as proud? And I had a right to feel proud; what I had planned and striven for unceasing, for nine days, I had at last achieved. I was a free man once more....

[Although Benson had escaped prison, difficulty beset him on every hand as he sought to get back to the South.]

Having swum a last stretch, I found myself amongst fallen trees, cut for fuel, and had much difficulty getting through them, for the broken twigs were constantly piercing my feet, in the fresh cuts, so that every step was exceedingly painful. Coming out of the woods into a field, I saw two horses, and tried to catch one, but could not. Seeing a house on a hill, I went toward it. Near one of the outhouses I found an old pair of shoes, but they were so large and hard and stiff, (having lain out in the sun and rain till nearly rotten), that I could not bear them on my feet. I ought to have soaked the shoes in water and worn them wet. I got into a small road and continued in it till it entered a larger, public road. Again I tried to capture a horse in a field, but after having his heels flourished around my head once or twice I concluded to leave him alone in his glory. Near daybreak May 26 I was walking in a lane, when I came up to two horses feeding. By approaching cautiously, I caught one. He was facing the right way, and I sprang on his back. But no sooner was I mounted than he whisked around and carried me back at a gallop the way I had come. Having no bridle, I tugged at his mane, and growled "Whoa!" but in vain; faster sped the nocturnal steed and his [k]nightly rider. I did not dare to jump off, at this speed, my feet being already so badly hurt, and I had about resigned myself to the role of Mazeppa, when an idea struck me. I reached forward, seized his ear and gave it a wrench. He stopped. So did I. But whether I dismounted on one side or in front, quietly in haste, I respectfully decline to state. I now retraced my steps, "a wiser if not a better man."

Just beyond where I had caught my Tartar, I saw before me, at some distance, the masts of a schooner. I knew this must be in the Potomac which is here about eight miles wide. So I turned off to the right, through a large gate opening into a field, and walked a short distance. Feeling by this time very tired, I sat down in a fence corner. A little Negro boy and girl came by, and seeing me, stopped and looked all the astonishment they must have felt. They carried pails and went into a cowpen hard by to milk. It was now near sunrise. I went to the cowpen and began talking with the little Negroes to learn, if possible, whether there were any Southern sympathizers about. Addressing the girl, I asked: "Where do you live?" She pointed to the house, a nice-looking dwelling, at some distance. . . . "Is your master in favor of the South?" "He was, but he ain't now." "How do you know?" "I hear him talking about it." "Are all the people that were in favor of the South changed?" "Most all of 'em." "Who are not changed?" "Well, there's Mr.———." "Where does he live?". . . . "How large a family has Mr.———?" "He hasn't got any; he lives by himself." "Is he rich?" "Yes, sir; he's a heap richer than my master." Taking another hearty drink of milk, I went away. If I could rely (and I thought I could) on the girl's statements, I was in fine luck; here was a man rich, living alone, a Southern sympathizer. I would go to him, tell him my case and ask help. I followed the direction given me, and came to the house. . . . It was old, weatherbeaten, in the last stages of dilapidation;—no rich man lived *there*. It may be that I had misunderstood my directions. I passed on with a heavy heart. The disappointment was very great. . . .

About the middle of the day the rain ceased and the sun came out. I stopped in a fence corner, and pulling off my jacket to dry, I lay down and slept some. I waked in the evening, feeling hungry. Looking out in the field, I saw two small boys. I put on my jacket and went to them, and asked them whether they had seen a stray horse that day, giving a description of one I pretended to be looking for. They had not. I shifted the conversation gradually to the war, and was told by them that three men in the neighborhood were Southern sympathizers, one especially so; his house they pointed out in the distance. I left them, going as though in another way, but out of their sight I turned and went to the house. A lady, I suppose his wife, being in the room with the man, I hesitated to state my case before her, so I made inquiry as to the horse again, saying I had followed him farther than I had expected and was hungry, and asked if he would be so kind as to give me a little something to eat.

He asked the lady to get something for me, and as soon as she stepped out of the room I told the man the truth. At once he said he was a Union man, and that he could give me nothing to eat. I asked him not to inform upon me. He answered that there was no one nearer than the Point to inform; that he was unwell, and shouldn't go there.

So I left, dinnerless and disheartened. I walked very fast for a long time, to get clear of the neighborhood. As I went, I reflected upon the circumstance, and I made a firm resolve

not to betray myself to anyone again. This resolution I rigidly
adhered to, though how nearly tempted sometimes to tell,
my recital will make evident. I think now that I made
a mistake in not having bestowed confidence somewhere;
but chafing as I was then with the rejection of it and with
the keen disappointment, and dreading lest another time I
might be delivered up I resolved to trust solely to my own
individual exertions, which had so far liberated me. I said
"I will trust Berry Benson, and nobody else."

. . . It was now about sunrise of Friday, May 27, 1864. Now
and then a cart would go by. . . . Hearing a horse coming
from toward the town I looked up. There he rode, the man
I had been all along on the lookout for,—a Federal cavalryman, fully armed and equipped. I lay low and watched. . . . I
would leave that road and keep to the woods. My traveling
now became very painful. I was always stepping on stones
and dead branches which gave me great pain . . . I continued
to walk till about noon,—then I came to a little field, in
which I saw a Negro woman and her two children hoeing
near their cabin. I decided to venture, so I went to her and
asked about the stray horse. Of course she hadn't seen it.
I asked whether she could give me something to eat. She
said yes, and asked me to her cabin. She fried a rasher or
two of bacon, and placed it before me with some cold corn-
bread and cold coffee. Had my eyes been shut I might possibly have been able to tell, by the feel in my mouth, which
was bread and which was meat, but not by the taste, for my
taste was gone, with my forty-eight hours' fast. Although I
ate heartily I tasted nothing, until, near the close of the
meal, I began to taste the bacon grease into which I was
dipping my bread, having eaten all the meat. During my
eating the woman had told me she was a Catholic, and
that her husband, though temporarily absent, was afraid
to go abroad much, his life having been threatened by a

neighbor. Having finished eating, I thanked my black hostess, and bade her goodbye, which I did very hastily, as I felt that the victuals would not rest upon my stomach. . . .

Having now shoes and stockings [a young farmer had given him some], I stopped at the first stream I came to, and washed my feet well and long, picking the sand out from the cuts with a needle, and greasing them with some of the fat bacon the lady gave me in the morning. I also washed my shoes of the mud, and greased them to make them soft. Then I put them on and they fit me nicely. Oh, how proud I felt! and how comfortable! Then I washed my face and combed my hair. Then I stuck my thumbs in my armholes, cocked my hat to one side, planted my right foot out at an angle, and winked one eye,—such a high and mighty swell! Isn't a soldier a ridiculous thing? After resting awhile I ate a little of the food I had, and shuffled on, no longer barefoot, but the shoes hurt my sore feet some, of course. Traveling the road, I met a carriage, in which were some ladies, returning from church, I suppose. As I passed they looked at me with considerable attention, (I am by no means vain) which seemed to deepen into marked interest, (I say I am not at all vain) and then, as I lifted my hat with a graceful bow, they—(I tell you I am *not* vain),—they bowed! To me, a poor, ragged, dirty devil, whose only claim to recognition from them was, I well know now, the gray jacket that I wore. And why did I not stop, do you ask, and say, "Ladies, I am in trouble; I belong to Lee, and I am trying to get back to him; can you not help me?"—I had said I would not, and everybody says I am obstinate. . . .

[May 30, 1864] Learning now, by asking, that I was within twenty miles or less of Washington, I determined to go to the river and see how things looked. . . . I saw it, with schooners and other small vessels in it, both in motion and at anchor. I kept on up the river going over many hills, high

and steep. About 3 P.M. I climbed a tall chestnut tree on
the top of one of the highest hills to take a survey. This tree
appeared to be, or to have been, used as a lookout; for leaning against its lowest limb was a cedar pole about twenty
feet long, the branches being cut off to within a few inches
of the body so as to make a natural ladder. When I reached
the top I had a fair view of the river, which was very wide.
I could see vessels of many kinds and sizes going up and
down. Up the river on the opposite side, I saw a city. This
I knew must be Alexandria. To the right of it, and seeming
to rise out of the river was a monument. This was the unfinished Washington monument. Farther to the right, loom-
ing above the tops of the trees, was a great white dome;
the dome of the Capitol. I had often heard the *old* Capitol
Prison talked about, and I now thought to myself, maybe I
will soon be there a prisoner.

[In order to prevent becoming a prisoner, Benson decided
on a new tactic—he would swim the Potomac to Washington
and hope for some way of escape there.]

But the thought of recapture was too distressing, and I
shut it out of my mind. I had a comfortable seat on a limb,
and now and then I caught myself nearly dozing. It was all
I could do to keep from going to sleep, yet I knew if I did
fall asleep I would fall out of the tree. This shows in what
a state of exhaustion I was from fatigue, lack of food, loss
of sleep, and strain of mind on the watch to guard against
surprise. . . . [He decided to swim the Potomac, and because
he was so weak and so near exhaustion he made a frame of
four fence rails to hold to as he floated across.] I aimed for
a point of woods on the opposite shore, but I expected the
current to drift me far below it. Fortunately, however, the
water seemed to be nearly still; it may be the tide was coming
up and so counteracted the current . . . I had got far out in
the river, my hands and feet both employed in swimming

when suddenly ... I saw a schooner with all sails set coming up the river, heading right toward me. Whether it would pass in front of me, or behind me, or over me I could not tell, but I imagined it rushing full tilt against me and burying me in the water. I could only await its approach with anxiety. I had the good fortune to see it pass behind me, though quite close. ...

Soon after this, cramp seized my left leg, and I will acknowledge to feeling a good deal of alarm, for the best swimmer may go under when caught with cramp. I kicked hard, and the cramp left me. Not long after, I saw a steamboat coming up the river, lit up from stern to stem with lights, white and red. It was a beautiful sight, as I was able to appreciate even then, when it seemed about to ride over me. But I had the satisfaction of seeing it too pass close behind me, while I rode up and down, up and down on the waves after it had gone by. This was my last danger. I soon began to draw near the point of woods I had been swimming for. After one or two trials, letting down my feet, I touched the bottom, and my long swim was over. Before quitting the water I untied my strings and put them in my pocket and shoved the rails out in the stream. Oh, what a thrill of joy went through me as my feet once more pressed the soil of Virginia! I was in my own country,—near Mt. Vernon, too, I knew. I climbed up a steep bank and went some distance into the woods to make a fire. I gathered some sticks, and tried a match. It was wet. I gave up the hope of having any fire tonight. I tried another. It lit. I soon had a low, hot fire, and lay down before it, taking off some of my clothes to dry them, and spreading open my Testament before it to dry the wet leaves. I slept some. When dawn came, I took up the line of march, my clothes not yet dry.

[Unfortunately, late that afternoon Berry met two boys, one of them an 18-year-old, carrying a gun, and told them he was looking for work. They took him to a miller nearby who soon discovered he was a Southern soldier and turned him over to the 8th Illinois Cavalry. Soon after his capture he was sent to Elmira Prison in New York. Again he escaped, by an ingeniously dug tunnel, and made his way back to Virginia. When he heard that Mosby's Raiders were active in that section, he determined to try to join them.]

... At length, a little after dark (Sunday, October 23, 1864) I saw a light from a house at some distance from the road,—so far that I thought nobody would be stopping there. On reaching the place, however, the owner had the same story to tell, no room, Mosby's men filled him up. I could sleep in the barn, I said. He made some excuse; said Mosby's men had the barn too, I believe; but I think the truth of the matter was he was afraid I might get off with some of the horses in the night. Finally he said he would see some of the men and if they said take me in he would do it. I suppose he considered himself "let" to Mosby's men for the night. He came back and told me to come in.

There were two young men sitting down by the fire, waiting for supper, while others outside busied themselves looking after their horses. The two young men looked up as I entered and took a seat before the fire and, as was natural, soon began to ask me questions about myself. The answers I gave shortly made it necessary for me to tell my whole story as briefly as possible, and when I had got through, I went on to tell them of meeting Ben Crowley and Sam Underwood and Woodhouse (or Waterhouse) at the Old Capitol. Now, the two men had listened to me all along without saying much, only now and then putting in a question, but when I mentioned these names, they at once began to talk, and told me very plainly that they had thought I was lying, had pretty well made up their minds that I was a spy, and had just as much made up their minds what they were going to do with me, but that they felt satisfied now that all I had said was true, from my knowing their men whom they knew to be prisoners. Then they called in the other men: "Boys, come in here; here's a man knows Ben Crowley, and Underwood, and the rest of the boys; was with 'em in the Old Capitol." And they all crowded round and asked a hundred questions; and the next thing I saw was a pulling out of pocket books, and a snug little sum was put into my hands. . . . But, indeed, I made but a slight protest, for I needed the money, and it was offered in such a free "you'd-do-just-the-same-by-me" kind of way, and with such soldierly sympathy for the rough time I'd had, that I would not have hurt their feelings by absolute refusal.

We had supper together, and at bedtime one of them insisted on giving me up his bed in the house under pretense that he wanted to sleep by his horse anyhow. I felt quite a desire to go on this raid, and said so, and the men said they'd see what could be done about it, but thought it would be a poor chance on account of the difficulty in procuring a horse. It was not far to go, the next morning, to the meeting-place, which I found to be at a blacksmith shop . . . and there were quite a number of the band already met. My new friends after a while came to tell me it was impossible to get a horse, so I had to suffer the disappointment. They introduced me to their chief, who kindly told me how I'd best proceed to avoid meeting the enemy's scouting parties, advising me to stick close to the mountains.

[Berry soon joyfully rejoined his old outfit and was reunited with his brother B. K. By this time the war was going very badly for the South, and the Confederate forces were disorganized and desperate. But not Berry Benson! His spirit was as undaunted as ever, and the following remarkable episode, in which he escaped capture himself and instead captured three Federals, is one of the most unforgettable of all those recorded in his story of the war.]

Whilst I was at the edge of the woods I was astounded to see, standing some thirty or forty yards from me . . . three of the enemy! And as I turned my head and saw them, they began beckoning to me with their hands to "come in." What a fix I was in! With an unloaded gun, and without a cartridge to load it, I had run right into the hands of three armed men who were now calling on me to surrender!

I never knew before how quick a man can think. For my first impulse, seeing the strait I was in, was to do as I was bid, throw down my gun and surrender. But, as I did, the thought of Elmira prison came to me, and with it the *feeling* of being in prison. I actually had the identical feeling that I had while a prisoner. And this feeling prompted me to take any risk—to run for it—close as I was they *might* miss me! And I was on the point of turning to run, when a third thought struck me—to play a bluff game and *capture them!*

In an instant I brought my gun up—I mean in an instant from the time I first perceived them and saw them beckoning, so swift were my thoughts, so swift that you could not say "Surrender—Run—Bluff 'em!" as quick as I acted. I threw my gun up in the position of ready, and called out: "Surrender! You are cut off and surrounded! Surrender!" They did not stir, but I saw I had alarmed them. They evidently thought they *might* be cut off from their line in the rear— and they stood irresolute.

This hesitation assured me of victory. I cried out: "Throw down your guns and surrender, or I will shoot you!" and I threw my gun to my shoulder. Down went two of their rifles and they came running toward me. The other still hesitated. I cried again: "If you don't throw down that gun, I'll shoot you!" and I took aim. Down went his gun, and he came also. With a heart overflowing with joy at my fortunate escape,

I put my prisoners in front of me and marched them to the rear, till I landed them safely with the Sharpshooters.

[Benson fires his last shot of the war and reviews in memory his part in following "the tattered flags of Jackson's battalions."]

. . . I have somehow kept it in my recollection as being on the 7th [of April] that we (the S.S's) sharpshooters were skirmishing with the enemy in an oak wood. Their onset was at first so heavy that our connecting sharpshooters on our right gave way and fell back a little, but we Carolinians kept our ground pretty well though the fire from the enemy was heavy. . . . Immediately in my front was a thin wood of bushes too open for the enemy to occupy. But after awhile I saw a puff of white smoke shoot out from the pines; I watched to see the man but could not, though once or twice again came the puff of smoke and the bullet singing by. Keeping close watch, so as to get a fair shot, I had the good fortune to see, directly, the dark figure of a man move his position a little, and stand, exposed from his waist upward above a pine bush. The distance was probably 150 yards. I leveled my rifle and fired, and when the smoke cleared away he had disappeared, whether struck or not I could not tell.

But the interest of this shot, and an abiding one, is that it was *my last shot in the war*. Two days more, and that long series of days of toil and exposure; hunger, cold, fatigue, and danger—days that seemed then as though they would never draw to an end—were over; and the warm sunshine in which we basked as we lay on winter noons by the side of our log cabins; the white moonshine of the nights that gleamed upon our rifle-barrels as we stood on our picket posts; the ring of rifle and axe; the tramp and rustle of thousands on the march; all these were to be no longer facts, and present consciousness, today's and tonight's; they were to become far-away yesterdays—were to fade out and backward into mere dim history. And while I write it seems as though now, in being obliged to say "It *was*," some great bundle of treasure-holding years have been torn out of my life—some sweet thing slipped out of my grasp—and, like a silver coin dropped into deep water, I see it slipping away, down, down, sparkling as it sinks, but ever growing dimmer, dimmer, until I fear me that ere I am hardly bemoaning my first gray hairs I shall have to bethink myself to say truly whether indeed I did share in the clash and struggle of a vigorous war; whether indeed I have seen painted red on the sky the tattered flags of Jackson's battalions. No, indeed, I am wrong; that magic name would even in death bear me back in spirit to the clover fields of Virginia—to the Valley and the turnpike—remembering how even *I* followed *him*.

. . . I fell into the practice of lying down whenever there was a halt, requesting to be waked when the column began to move, and so I got many a good little rest, and much badly-needed sleep, for it took but a moment to drop off to sleep. And so it was, day and night all one, till we reached Appomattox on the 9th.

[And now Berry Benson comes to that April day when Lee surrendered and the long four years of fighting ended. No doubt the great majority of less sensitive soldiers suffered less, but to him Appomattox brought all the pathos of a personal bereavement.]

Harassed on all sides by the enemy's cavalry, we the S.S's were often thrown out on the flank and had more or less skirmishing to do. Every hour brought news of the capture or burning of portions of our wagon trains, while wagons, broken down horses, pieces of artillery, stragglers, and all kinds of munitions of war were being abandoned to fall into the hands of our pursuers. A fusillade off at a distance would tell of a descent upon a wagon train by their cavalry,—then a column of smoke rising above the treetops would tell of its capture and destruction. Not much that was captured, however, was of service to the enemy, for we were too poor to own food, clothing, blankets or anything but powder and lead, and not enough of that. The horses were mere skeletons, and fell all along the road, dying out of sheer exhaustion and starvation, and the men were in not much better condition. Straggling became the rule, rather than the exception, and from sheer weakness and lack of sustenance; and many a brave man lagged then behind his command who had never lagged before. And the 8,000 who drew up that morning before Appomattox were not 8,000 bodies, it was 8,000 *souls*, which still dragged along with them their unwilling bodies, whether or no.

. . . Over to the left there was some fighting going on. The sharpshooters were ordered forward. We marched down across an open field to a stream some six yards wide perhaps, and we crossed on a plank or log which lay across it and formed on the other side, the enemy's ground,—and were about to continue the advance and make an attack, when, to our surprise we were recalled. We marched over to the big road, entering it near a house on the top of which floated a large yellow flag—the hospital flag. And as we marched back up the road to the brigade, we saw a queer sight. Through the field, close by the road, a piece of artillery was being driven, and the drivers and artillerymen accompanying were all Yankees! We didn't understand, but somebody said we had just captured the piece and its own men were being made to drive it in to our lines. Then I saw a Federal officer [This officer was General Custer.] come galloping in, carrying aloft a white handkerchief. What did this mean? Had we surrounded a small body of the enemy and were they about to surrender? But presently the whisper began to pass from mouth to mouth, that it was a flag of truce, and that *General Lee* was about to surrender. I remember with what surprise and utter discredit I heard the rumor. The thought had actually never entered my mind before, hard pressed as I knew we were. General Lee's army surrender! The idea was simply preposterous, and I hooted it. There had been surrenders and there would be surrenders, but not Lee's army!

The firing had all ceased, and we saw Confederate regiments returning from the field of battle,—and now the whole army (and a small one it was) gathered together on a low hill that lay over against Appomattox. And along the ridge of hills opposite were stretched the long dark lines of the enemy. They lay directly in our front, blocking our further retreat. We were drawn up in column of regiments, I believe, and ordered to stack arms; and then the rumor grew louder and more assured, that we were indeed about to surrender. I took alarm. We were not kept to our pieces, but were let wander about, resting under the trees, and there the enemy in full view. And no fighting anywhere.

I looked up Captain Barnwell (commander of Company H) and asked him what he knew. He *knew* nothing, but thought it not improbable General Lee was about to surrender. Then I looked up General McGowan and begged him to tell me whether he knew. He did not know, but—then I told him I would not stay if a surrender was to be made. I had been in prison once and I was not going again; I would make my way out and join General Johnston in North Carolina. He told me not to act hastily; but to wait until a surrender became certain, then if I would, to go. I talked with B. K. He was ready to follow me anywhere. I did not want many companions, and spoke to only one other; this was Bell, "old Cator." Yes, he would go with us anywhere, to Texas, if we said so. But 'Cator had a friend, Clarke (the same who went out with me, wounded, at the battle of Chancellorsville), who was a neighbor of Bell's at home, and whom Bell somewhat looked up to and thought very much of. Him he must tell goodbye. So Bell went off to the wagon train, where Clarke was (Clarke's wound had never since Chancellorsville allowed him to march and fight with the rest of us), and B. K. and I waited. Presently 'Cator returned, tears in his eyes, and declared that he could not make up his mind to leave Clarke, and as he was in great doubt as to what he ought to do, we all went together to Clarke, to talk about it; and the upshot of it was that Bell decided to remain with Clarke.

I ought to have said before this that I had gone again to General McGowan, to ask whether we were really going to surrender, and I found him in the woods, crying, half-dressed, taking off his old dirty uniform, and putting on a brighter, newer one, used on state occasions. I did not then need his acknowledgment of our miserable fate; his face and the changing of his uniform were proof enough. By that time it got to be well-known amongst the men that Lee had determined to surrender, and it was a lamentable spectacle then to see how the men took it. Some seemed to be glad that it was all over, but even they would, I have no doubt, have been as ready to charge as the rest. But mostly they were sad and gloomy faces. For myself, I cried; I could not help it. And all about were men crying, plenty of them. We left General McGowan crying, and Clarke and Bell also.

I went to Powell, told him I was going to escape if I could, and proposed his coming with me. But he declined. Then I asked him to give me his telescope rifle, but for some reason he declined this, too. I had in my pocket two dollars, a greenback bill Father had once sent me in a letter, and hearing it reported that the terms of the surrender stipulated parole for all privates and non-commissioned officers, but that commissioned officers would be sent to Northern prisons, I looked up Captain Barnwell and gave him the money.

He refused at first to take it, but I finally made him take it. I told him he would need it bad enough.

So B. K. and I left the little tattered, weary, sad and weeping army—*our* army—left them there on the hill with their arms stacked in the field, all in rows—never to see it any more. And oh, it was my sweetheart who was dead that day! My sweetheart whom I turned and went away from that day in April! Never any worse could I feel at parting forever from the white coffined face of a woman I loved, as at last we told Clarke and Bell goodbye, and crossed the road into the untenanted fields and thickets, and in a little while lost sight of all that told of the presence of that that was left of the army that through four long years had beaten back time after time its enemy, keeping Richmond safe and sound. And just as it was with me after my mother died, when every night I cried on my pillow till it seemed that my heart would break for the loss of her, so now again it was that night after night, as we lay in the woods to sleep, my jacket was wet with tears, folded under my head for a pillow. And so for many a night after.

CHAPTER THREE

War as It Came to Wives and Families at Home

My homespun dress is plain, I know,
My hat's palmetto, too;
But then it shows what Southern girls
For Southern rights will do.
We have sent the bravest of our land
To battle with the foe
And we will lend a helping hand—
We love the South you know.

"THE HOMESPUN DRESS" WAS ONE OF THE MOST POPULAR OF *all the war songs. It perhaps expresses a lighter-hearted attitude toward the sacrifices women had to make than many of them felt. For when the men left for the battlefields, women had to manage the corn and cotton fields. The desperate straits to which some women were often driven are described by Mrs. R. Balzer of Tennessee: "After my grandmother's husband entered the army her horse was stolen, and she hitched her two boys to the plow to make her garden."*

A similar story of a Mrs. Simmons is told by a corre-

spondent from Jasper County, Mississippi: "In 1863 Mrs. Sim-mons made 300 bushels of corn, 100 bushels of potatoes, and enough peas to fatten her hogs. She did the plowing herself with an old wind-broken pony. Her two little daughters, aged twelve and fourteen, did the hoeing. She also made 100 pounds of tobacco. After her crop was finished, she did weaving enough to buy her salt and a pair of cards [for spin-ning], and had some money left."

And Mrs. Jessie McDanield Hamrick of Georgia proudly tells a tale about her great-aunts: "While their husbands were serving in the Confederate army, two sisters, Mrs. Ann Stephenson Gillespie and Frances Scoggins, shared the same farmhouse in Carroll County, Georgia. Frances was delicate and therefore took as her duties housekeeping, cooking on the open fire, and caring for the children of both women. During the day she picked seed out of cotton, spun, knit, and sewed by hand. At night she was joined in these tasks by her sister Ann, a large and healthy person, who milked and plowed the cow, making the crop of corn, peas, cotton, vegetables, and fruit. She cared for and sheared the sheep, fed and butchered the hogs, plucked the geese, and cut wood for heat and cooking."

Walter L. Thomas, County Historian of Mitchell County, North Carolina, describes wartime conditions for women with this picture of Mrs. Aaron Thomas:

She with a large number of small children was compelled to cultivate her corn crop at night by the light of the moon. There were just not enough daylight hours in the day for her to do all the tasks that must be done and still cultivate her crop. She would get all the children to bed and to sleep, and then go out to the fields to work at night. Despite this arduous manual labor, provisions were so scarce that she and her children survived only by the desperate expedient of serving two meals a day instead of the customary three. She and the children became so accustomed to the two-meal-per-day regime that after the war was over and provisions had become plentiful they never really enjoyed the third meal again.

During the war this mother had saved her soldier husband's pay to buy a place for themselves when the war was over, and on his return from service all that she could present him was a bundle of worthless Confederate money.

Young boys, inexperienced and unsure of themselves, also had to tackle the management of farms or sometimes of large plantations. The following letter asking for farming advice was written by a 16-year-old to his older brother in the army. It was sent to us by Mrs. George S. Baker of North Carolina.

Lake of the Woods
Sunday, Nov. 3rd, 1861

Dear Brother,

I have in a measure taken your place at home, and you know I never cared anything about the farm before, and your advice and experience would be very beneficial and acceptable to me. So if you should have any time I would be very much pleased if you would write to me. . . . I reckon you know better what advice I need than I do. . . .

We commenced gathering peas before the 24th of September, and we have been gathering every opportunity since. . . .

Yours &c.
T. E. Davis

This boy, a year later, ran away to join the army and was killed in action in 1864.

Hard, unaccustomed work, sacrifice, and death: all had to

*be faced by Southern women. But grief over the loss of sons
was of course not limited to the South, and sometimes the
mutual sympathy of women in this plight caused old feelings
of enmity to vanish. The mother of the young farmer who
wrote the foregoing letter lost her son Weldon in November,
1863, and while she grieved over his death on the battlefield,
the following letter reached her from across enemy lines:*

Washington City
Dec. 8, '63

Mrs. Edward Davis, Warrenton, N.C.
Dear Madam:

In the discharge of a most painful duty, I address you,
sympathizing most truly in the sore affliction which it has
pleased God to appoint you. Your son, Captain Weldon Ed-
wards Davis, was wounded and captured at Kelly's Ford,
Va., on the 8th of Nov. On the 9th he was brought to this
city & placed in the Douglas Hospital, receiving the most
careful attention and provision. Capt. Davis's wound, a
severe fracture of the right leg, rendered amputation necessary. At first surgeons were hopeful, but on the 19th symp-
toms of tetanus appeared, rendering unavailing all skill and
attention of the surgeons in his behalf. He expired Sunday
the 22nd.

I was permitted to visit him every day, was with him the
whole of the last day of his life, witnessed his baptism, his
holy & happy death, and received his last message to you,
his dear mother, assuring you that he died a Christian in the
hope of a glorious immortality. I attended his funeral in the
cemetery of the soldiers' home. At his request, the effects
found on his person when captured are in my hand to be
delivered to you.

With sincerest respect, your fellow sufferer,
MRS. ELIZABETH BLOUNT

Months later Mrs. Davis learned more about the death of her son Weldon through a soldier who was with him when he fell. And so she wrote another son in the army how a Union soldier attempted to help the wounded Confederate— and the terrible cost of this kind act:

Sunday, June 25, 1864

Dear Burwell,

... Wms. has been exchanged, and is gone back. He told some particulars in regard to Weldon. He says they all surrendered except Weldon, and he tried to escape and was fired on, and that was the only shot fired at them. He said when Weldon fell a Yankee officer galloped up to him and said, "Captain, I am sorry to see you so badly wounded. Have something to drink; it will help you," and handed him his canteen, which he took and drank of its contents, when one of our men fired at this officer, and he fell by Weldon's side.

R. P. D.
[Rebecca P. Davis]

Mrs. C. E. Means of South Carolina wrote the following story that gives another example of Northern kindness in the face of Southern tragedy—a quality which appeared more frequently in letters and records we have received than many people today would think possible:

Aunt Kate was born in 1826 in Cherokee County, South Carolina. ... Her husband was among the very first volunteers to fight for the Confederacy. She suffered acutely from the separation, but at once identified herself with the work to be done for her country.

In December, 1864, Aunt Kate received a letter ... a scrawl, broken and tremulous ... but she knew it was her husband's: "I am exchanged; have been at Fort Donaldson. From the cruelty, cold, and starvation encountered there I am nearly dead. Come to Savannah to meet me. I may, God willing, live to see you once more."

Aunt Kate at once hired a conveyance and drove through to Savannah where she finally found the building used as a hospital for the sick Confederates. Finding no one in authority, she decided to walk through the rows of cots and search for her husband. It was a heart-breaking sight. The poor exchanged men were as ghastly as rags, filth, sores, and starvation could make humanity.... One poor man she noticed who was so emaciated he seemed a living skeleton. One eye was eaten out by scurvy; the other closed as if he were asleep, but his face was filled with pain. She passed on a few steps, growing sick with apprehension that her husband might be like one of these. Overcome by a sudden faintness she leaned on a nearby pillar for support.

Standing there, trembling, depressed, and discouraged she heard her name spoken in faint tones.

"Kate! Kate!" It was the man she had thought was asleep. She looked back at the cot and saw the wasted hand of her husband held out entreatingly to her. . . .

The sick man's constant prayer was to see his children again, and his wife determined he should. She went to the Federal commander and asked for transportation for her ill husband who was an exchanged prisoner. Not only did the Federal general give her an order to pass the lines and transportation to Port Royal, but also sent an ambulance to carry them to the wharf and detailed two soldiers to help them on board.

Although Aunt Kate lost her husband, she always remembered that in her sore hour of need she received help and sympathy from the highest officers to the common Yankee soldier.

The women of the South willingly gave for their cause the things that meant most to them. They gave up their husbands and sons, not grudgingly, but with Spartan courage. The following letter is a moving example of this patriotism. A Clark County, Virginia, woman whose husband had been two years in Yankee prisons and in exile from his home, and whose son (an only child, in his eighteenth year) was then in some Northern Bastille as a prisoner of war, wrote to her husband:

If it were possible, I should like you to be at home; but I do not want you or O. ever to give up the struggle for liberty and our rights. . . . I would love to be with you; but do not expect it in these times. I wish O. was at home—I mean in his company; but I would rather he would be a prisoner for the war than have him at home dodging his duty, as some do. I am proud to think every man in my little family is in the army. If I have but two, they are at their post of duty.

On the other hand some women with half-starving children so desperately needed their husbands that they urged them to desert. An old schoolbook, Moore's School History of North Carolina, *contains a paragraph in illustration of this point which many a schoolboy (including the writer) remembered long after he forgot other dates and facts of his history lessons:*

My Dear Edward:

I have always been proud of you, and since your connection with the Confederate army I have been prouder of you than ever before. I would not have you do anything wrong for the world, but before God, Edward, unless you come home, we must die. Last night I was aroused by little Eddie's crying. I called and said, "What is the matter, Eddie?" And he said, "O mamma, I am so hungry." And Lucy, Edward, your darling Lucy, she never complains but she is growing thinner and thinner every day. And before God, Edward, unless you come home, we must die.

Your Mary

Edward did desert—and this letter from his wife was given to the court as the only evidence he could offer when tried by court martial for desertion. Although he voluntarily returned to his command after his family was provided for, the court martial found him guilty but recommended mercy. So he remained in service and was last seen, pale and bloody, firing after the retreating Federals. He then fell dead at his post in battle.

The war swept thousands of women and children from their homes as described so vividly by Mrs. McGuire in her diary (see Chapter 8, p. 149). But some stayed at home because they had nowhere else to go. They were often in physical danger themselves, and sometimes risked their lives to help soldiers. In November, 1863, Miss Belle Norris was in her home at Culpeper Courthouse, Virginia, when the Yankee army advanced on that town. As it is told in a book of long ago, The Civil War in Song and Story, *"it was the scene of quite a brisk fight— especially was the artillery firing heavy. During the fight, one of our wounded heroes between the fire of friend and foe was seen by Miss Norris whose tender sympathies were deeply aroused in his behalf. Having resolved to save him, she rushed from her house, regardless of her own safety, between the combatants, amid shot and shell, raised him bleeding from the dust, and had almost succeeded in gaining a place of safety, when (our forces having fallen back) a Yankee officer rode up, and*

being struck by her patriotism, dismounted and helped her
carry her wounded countryman into the house."

Another heroine was 14-year-old Emma Sansom of Geor-
gia and later of Texas. Ray H. Greene of the Gilmer Mirror,
Gilmer, Texas, wrote the following story of how Emma
earned the title, "The Sunbonnet Heroine."

She is buried in Little Mound Church Cemetery fifteen
miles west of Gilmer, Texas. The inscription on a tall white
stone marker spins the clock back to a May morning in 1863.
It reads: "E.S.J.—Girl Heroine Who Piloted Gen. Forrest
Across Black Creek and Enabled Him to Capture Gen.
Streight."

This is the resting place of Emma Sansom Johnson.
A large granite monument, however, stands in downtown
Gadsden, Alabama, and in that same city a large high school
is called the Emma Sansom High School in her memory.

As a 14-year-old farm girl on May 2, 1863, Emma took her
fling at glory. General Abel D. Streight was leading a Federal force across Northern Alabama headed for a large Confederate supply depot at Rome, Georgia. Hot in pursuit was
General Nathan Bedford Forrest, the cavalryman who believed in getting there "fustest with the mostest." It was a
100-mile-long running battle.

Two miles from Gadsden, General Streight crossed the
swollen waters of Black Creek, then set fire to the wooden
bridge. Quickly thereafter General Forrest galloped up, saw
the situation, then raced to the nearby Sansom farmhouse.
Emma told the General of a ford she had seen cattle cross
and she volunteered to serve as a guide. General Forrest
swung her up behind his saddle and the two rode through a
hail of rifle fire from the Federal rear guard covering the
burning bridge. Bullets pierced Emma's skirt, but she waved
her sunbonnet in defiance. General Forrest's men found

and used the ford to which Emma directed them, overtook General Streight, captured his men, and for the time ended the threat to the Rome, Georgia, supply depot.

The Confederate Congress struck a gold medal in Emma's honor, and the Alabama legislature voted her a section of land. She married an Alabama soldier in 1864 when she was 15 or 16. Hard times hit after the war, and in 1876 they left Alabama for Texas, settling in Upshur County, where she reared five sons and two daughters, and died August 9, 1900.

Not all Southern women were heroines, however. Some who may have indeed suffered much themselves did not sympathize deeply enough with the men who had suffered far more. Such an incident occurred when a group of women taunted some long besieged soldiers of Vicksburg for retreating. Mrs. Mary Loughborough's My Cave Life in Vicksburg, *published in 1864, tells of a group of women who upon hearing sounds of horsemen and rattling wagons rushed out to see what was happening:*

"What can be the matter?" we all cried, as the streets and pavements became full of these worn and tired-looking men. We sent down to ask, and the reply was: "We are whipped and the Federals are after us."

"Where are you going?" we asked.

An embarrassed, pained look came over some of the faces that were raised to us. At last one man looked up in a half-surly manner, and answered: "We are running."

"Shame on you all!" cried some of the ladies across the street, becoming excited.

I could not but feel sorry for the poor worn fellows, who did seem indeed heartily ashamed of themselves; some without arms, having probably lost them in the first break of the companies.

"We are disappointed in you!" cried some of the ladies. "Who shall we look to now for protection?"

At dark the fresh troops from Warrenton marched by. . . . The ladies waved their handkerchiefs, cheering them, and crying:

"These are the troops that have not run. You'll stand by us and protect us, won't you! You won't *retreat* and bring the Federals behind you."

And the men, who were fresh and lively, swung their hats and promised to die for the ladies—never to run—never to retreat; while the poor fellows on the pavement, sitting on their blankets, lying on the ground, leaning against trees, or anything to rest their wearied bodies, looked on silent and dejected.

No story of Southern women in the Civil War would be complete without mention of a romance whose details were sent the writer by M. L. Fleetwood, publisher of the Tribune News, Cartersville, Georgia. *This refers to the romance of young William Tecumseh Sherman, then a cadet at West Point, and one of the academy's most beautiful and charming visitors, Miss Cecilia Stovall of Augusta, Georgia.*

Strongly documented Georgia tradition says that young Sherman asked for her hand but was refused. Miss Stovall returned to her Augusta home and gave her heart to Charles Shellman of Cherokee County. He built for her a magnificent home, "Etowah Heights," on the Etowah River. In this home she reigned as a queen, gracefully and charmingly. In 1864 when Sherman marched through Georgia, burning as he went, he recalled this unforgotten romance of his early youth and ordered his men not to destroy the beautiful home in which Cecilia Stovall then lived and to which she had brought many priceless portraits of her ancestors and objects from trips abroad.

The war would be over in '63, they said. But it stretched on and on and the longer it lasted the more deeply the South was invaded. Southerners never forgot the Yankee raids. Many a grandchild has been spellbound by tales such as these that follow of Southern courage in facing the enemy, or Southern shrewdness in outwitting the enemy. This recollection, for instance, is told by now 80-year-old Mrs. Rhydonia Pelham Burke of Alabama:

My father was one of the pioneer Baptist preachers of the state. One Saturday night when he was away from home at one of his churches, Mother waked up us children, saying, "Get up and dress quickly as the Yankees are coming." She had in her possession a Confederate flag which she told us to hide for fear that the house would be raided, and she put in my little homespun apron $100 in gold pieces.

The Federals later claimed they would have passed by in peace, but one of the home guards fired on them, and then the battle began. During the fray our Grandmother Pelham came from her house along to our home, calmly smoking her pipe, and went from house to house reassuring the frightened women and children. Henry Cain, a fine young man of the home guard, was killed, and a horse was shot down and the Yankee rider's leg was broken. When they had gone, Uncle Reddock Peacock came down the road with a tallow candle lit, hunting the dead and wounded.

They captured three of our men, but when morning came their wounded soldier had become so ill they released our men, bidding them call a doctor and care for their man. Uncle Daniel Cumbie took him to his house where they amputated his limb, but he soon died and was buried an unknown soldier in a nameless grave in old Asbury Church yard.

A few years afterward I married a Confederate veteran, and now I am nearing my eighty-first milestone. But the excitement of that night of war and the tramp, tramp of the horses' feet, the clanking of the swords, the firing of the guns in our sleepy village, together with the look of terror on that lovely, beautiful, youthful face of my mother, made such an impression that time has never erased it from my memory.

Another story is told by H. B. Wooley of Florida as it was handed down to him from his grandmother, Mary A. Wooley. This story, by the way, contains a rare reference to improper advances made on a Southern woman by a Federal soldier. We often think of rape as being almost inevitable in a war where one country is invaded by another. Possibly the very fact that this was a civil war kept the incidence of rape at such a low figure it was practically unheard of. At least it is interesting to note that out of hundreds of letters sent the writer on the Civil War, not once is rape mentioned. On the contrary, notice how the soldier Mrs. Wooley mentions was treated by his own men:

About mid-afternoon Friday, November 25, 1864, three Union soldiers arrived on horseback. After making a quick search of house and yard, two of them stood guard about the yard while the other one went back down the road. Soon a dozen or more arrived on horseback and proceeded with a more thorough search of the house; emptying all trunks, boxes, closets, and taking the bed mattresses and pillows into the yard, cutting open the ticks and scattering the contents. . . .

During these two days I saw "foragers" leave with empty wagons to return with loads of hay, grain, bacon, syrup, potatoes, etc. I saw our only milk cow and her calf slaughtered and cooked, as well as all our chickens, geese, and the three pigs we had fattened in a pen for next year's bacon. . . .

But the men were most courteous and gentlemanly to us. Only once a soldier passing me with an armload of wood for the fire made an improper pass toward me. He was immediately escorted from the house by an officer and I never saw him again.

No woman could have been cooler in the face of the most desperate danger than Addie Belcher whose story is told by Mrs. Troy L. Moran of Collinsville, Virginia:

My great-great-grandparents, Benjamin and Addie Belcher, were good old country Virginians living alone because their son who had been working in Ohio had been drafted into the Union army and upon contracting smallpox kept there in a hospital. Hence my great-great-grandparents were often at the mercy of deserters or stragglers.

One day a group of Union stragglers rode into Benjamin's yard, got off their horses and demanded that he get them what money, gold, or anything of value he had. He refused, saying he had nothing of value they would want. Not believing him they decided to force him to help them. One got a rope, threw it over the limb of an apple tree, and tied the other end around Benjamin's neck. They would pull him off the ground and hold the rope until he gasped for breath, then let him down and repeat their demands. Getting the same answer they would pull him up again. My great-great-grandfather had been pulled up the third time when my great-great-grandmother, observing what was taking place from her kitchen, knew something had to be done. So she opened the door and walked deliberately to where they were, looked up at Benjamin gasping for breath on the rope, and in a soft, calm voice said: "Benjamin, dinner is ready." Then turning to the Yankee stragglers she said in the same courteous, soft voice, "We would be much obliged if you would have dinner with us, too." The Yankee stragglers were so taken by surprise they let Benjamin down! To half-starved men not even a hanging can take the place of food. They all ate and rode off—but they did take Benjamin's four good horses and left four poor, half-starved horses in their place.

The next two very short tales of Yankee raids show how a little ingenuity made life much easier for families at home during the war. The first is told by Mrs. H. L. Stickler of Virginia of a woman who outwitted some Yankee soldiers:

The soldiers came to her poverty-stricken home and made a thorough search for food. Finally, after much fruitless rummaging they came upon her most prized possession—a can of lard. The officer snapped out a command about having it taken to their quarters.

The distressed woman said very sadly, "I just don't know what in the world I shall do about making soap now." The officer asked, "Madam, do you mean you would make soap of this fine lard?" She answered, "When the hog died of cholera I knew we couldn't eat the meat, so I cut it up and dried it down for lard, to make soap-grease."

Of course, the hog had not had cholera.

Mrs. Clint Bearden of Georgia relates an amusing story: "My grandmother had a good many beehives when the war was going on. She lived in a little one-room log house with just one door. She set the beehives in the front yard, took some cotton she had for making clothing, and spun a big cord and tied it to the beehives. When she saw the blue-

*coats coming she turned the beehive over with the cord
which she had pulled through a hole in the door. Several
times the horses and men got stung badly. The horses would
sometimes throw their riders and hurt them. But the men
always left her home without bothering her or what little
food she had!"*

*Sometimes, according to Mrs. Jean White of South Caro-
lina, it was the Yankees who showed humor and imagination:*

Not even Old Brick Church was spared by the grim for-
tunes of war. In order to rebuild a nearby bridge which had
been destroyed a few days previously by retreating Confederates, the invaders tore out the flooring and sleepers of
the Church. Still visible today is the pencilled apology of
a Northerner whose conscience must have bothered him
slightly. Written on the facing of the west doorway are these
words:

"Citizens of this community, please excuse us for defacing
your house of worship so much. It was absolutely necessary
to effect a crossing over the creek, as the Rebs destroyed the
bridge.   A YANKEE."

*The greatest cruelties of the war are reported as not from
enemy soldiers but from marauding outlaw bushwhackers.
In a diary dated 1863-64, Adeline McDowell Deaderick
wrote the following account which was sent us by her great-
granddaughter, Mrs. M. P. Burns of Alabama:*

The bushwhackers had watched one of our neighbors'
houses and knew that young Fisk Harris was at home. When
they began their attack, they broke the windows with a
fence rail and broke open the doors. Fisk heard the noise
and hurriedly ran to the garret, leaving his revolver on a
table at his bedside. They soon, with demoniacal yells, dis-

covered his hiding place and dragged him, half clad, through his mother's room. That sick mother cried and prayed and supplicated for her boy, but on they went, pell-mell, into the yard with his four sisters following, one keeping close to her brother to protect him. They rudely ordered her aside and shot him in their midst. After he fell they shot nine balls into him, looked a moment to see if he was dead, and dashed from the yard. The girls dragged the poor fellow into the house near where the mother lay, too terror stricken to say one word. Their strength was inadequate to lift him from the floor and there he lay in a pool of blood. Life was not extinct when they got him in; he recognized his mother's voice, but never spoke. Thus passed away one of the best boys I ever knew, just eighteen, and thus he was lying when I reached the house on that long remembered morning.

One of the worst experiences of families at home was Sherman's march, and the "bummer" outlaws who came with him. Naturally Southerners described this hideous climax of the war in searing words, but Northern newsmen were often equally as appalled as is shown in this first-hand description of a "bummer" written by a correspondent of the New York Herald:

Any man who has seen the object that the name [bummer] applies to will acknowledge that it was admirably selected. Fancy a ragged man, blackened by the smoke of many a pine-knot fire, mounted on a scraggy mule, without a saddle, with a gun, a knapsack, a butcherknife and a plug hat, stealing his way through the pine forests far out on the flanks of a column—keen on the scent of rebels, or bacon, or silver spoons, or corn, or anything valuable, and you have him in mind. Think how you would admire him if you were a lone woman, with a family of small children, far from help, when he blandly inquired where you kept your valuables. Think how you would smile when he pried open your chests with his bayonet, or knocked to pieces your tables, pianos, and chairs, tore your bed-clothing in three-inch strips, and scattered them about the yard. The "bummers" say it takes too much time to use keys. Colour is no protection from these roughriders. They go through a Negro cabin, in search of diamonds and gold watches, with just as much freedom and vivacity as they "loot" the dwelling of a wealthy planter. . . . There are hundreds of these mounted men with the column, and they go everywhere. Some of them are loaded down with silverware, gold coin, and other valuables. I hazard nothing in saying three-fifths (in value) of the personal property of the counties we have passed through were taken by Sherman's army.

As the war drew to a close, hunger crept across the Southland. Mrs. G. A. Simpson of South Carolina wrote:

One of the most interesting things I remember hearing my grandmother tell was about how the country people became so hungry for salt. After Sherman's march of destruction they dug up the dirt floor in the smokehouse, boiled it, and used the water to cook with. She said she had to ride on the boat from Camden, S. C., to Charleston to get a peck of meal, the trip taking two days. Rations were issued to the ones that had everything destroyed but they seldom got anything but meal and sometimes a little black molasses. Even their garden seed was destroyed. The people wouldn't plow their gardens the following year, afraid they might cover up some little vegetable plant or seed. They went over the garden with a short handled hoe, looking for and working carefully each little plant that came up.

And Mrs. Roy Plum of Arkansas relates, "We had an old timer in our community who says one of his most vivid recollections was his mother hitching him and some of the other children to the plow and trying to plow up a small plot of ground to raise a few vegetables for the family table. The family owned no horse. Couldn't have fed it through the winter, had they owned one. It was hungry times . . . those days. In fact, said Uncle Carroll, hunger to a lot of folks was even more frightening than the shooting war itself."

According to Mrs. A. M. Lyons of Texas, the invasion of Richmond was a catastrophe to Southern adults but the children loved to watch the Yankee troops pass down the streets while they (the children) would sing:

Wrap me in a Rebel flag and lay me by Jeff Davis,
Give my love to General Lee and kiss the rebel ladies.

CHAPTER FOUR

Colonel L. L. Polk's
Wartime Letters to His Wife

PERHAPS NOWHERE ELSE DID CONFEDERATE SOLDIERS EXPRESS *themselves so freely as in letters to their wives back home. And few Confederates became more famous in later life than Colonel L. L. Polk. He was North Carolina's first Commissioner of Agriculture and founded* The Progressive Farmer *in 1886. He is called "The Father of N.C. State College" because of his leadership in the 1885-87 fight for a separate land grant college. In 1889-1892 he headed the most powerful farm organization of the century, the 2-million-member National Farmers Alliance, winning in that position such farmer loyalty and confidence as was exemplified in an early 1892 remark of the Kinston, North Carolina,* Free Press: *"Some Alliancemen seem to have more confidence in Colonel Polk than in God!" He would almost certainly have been nominated for the Presidency in 1892 by the newly formed Agrarian People's Party if he had lived three months longer.*

In 1860 and early 1861 he opposed secession. But when Lincoln called on North Carolina for troops to fight its sister Southern states he said, "I am now for resistance to the bitter end." He helped train the militia of his county as col-

onel till May, 1862, then (at age 25) joined the regular army. His young wife, married at 17, as was typical of so many other Southern women of the 1860s, was barely 22 when left with two infant daughters to manage as well as the home, the plantation, crops, stock, and slaves. (Later she inherited ownership of The Progressive Farmer *and was its owner when the writer became editor in 1899.)*

Certainly Polk's letters reveal a wide variety of experiences. We find him thrilled by a close view of General Lee, next fighting and wounded at Gettysburg, then unable to conquer that common but unwelcome comrade of soldiers, the itch. About the latter he no doubt agreed with a poet of the period who wrote:

> In fine I know not which
> Can play the most deceitful game
> The devil, sulphur, or the itch—
> The three are but the same!

First we turn to a bit of suspense-filled war drama. Colonel Polk (who was always battling for some friendless underdog) made a fight with his officers to save a soldier he thought unfairly under death sentence as a deserter. Doggedly calling on them for reprieve or pardon, Polk reports these results: "The prisoner was placed in the ambulance with his coffin and escorted by a guard to the spot where his newly-made grave told him he was to be its permanent occupant. . . . He was placed out in front—his own company drawn up before him, the death sentence read to him—and then his reprieve!" So was the poor man saved from the firing squad of unwilling comrades, and Polk added: "I am proud I had anything to do with his release." Other deserters were not so fortunate, as an 1863 letter and others remind us: "Yesterday I had to witness the execution of two deserters."

"Were you at Gettysburg?" is one question most Confederates heard after 1865. In that historic struggle Polk fought and was wounded but made light of the matter in a July, 1863, letter: "I was in the terrible ordeal of the 1st, 2nd and 3rd insts. at Gettysburg, Pa. I am wounded, though happy to inform you that it is not serious. . . . I was struck to the ground, but recovered and went through the charge and was not sensible of the character of the wound until we all stopped."

"Did you ever see General Lee?" is another question many surviving Confederates were always asked. Polk did and in a letter describes his great commander as seen seated on "Traveler" December 9, 1863: "Yesterday we had our Corps reviewed by General Lee. I took a good look at the illustrious hero. He was certainly born to command. He is about six feet tall, weighs about 190, finely proportioned, perfectly erect, and sits a saddle with the ease and grace which is seldom commanded by our younger and prouder commanders. His manly and military bearing, his face covered with grey whiskers, his dark keen eyes make one feel that he is a man of no ordinary character or intellect."

One can find in the Polk letters some glimpse of war in nearly all its varying aspects: war in which men cheered an order for an almost sure death by bayonet-assault on a strongly entrenched bridge, a war in which unworthy leaders sometimes imperiled the lives of privates ("If I had the power I would reduce to ranks any officer who would get drunk in the presence of the enemy and thus wantonly sacrifice the lives of our brave men"). From a June 9, 1864, letter: "We have slept on the same ground three nights for the first time since April 14. I have not pulled off my clothes to sleep since that time and over half the time I sleep with boots on." To this June 9 letter, however, Polk added: "All in good health and cheerful and buoyant." As late as August and September, 1864, he reported soldiers "laughing and frolicking" in spite of the almost certain defeat that so many saw ahead. Then a letter about his unwelcome service as a conscript officer: "To ride up to a man's door, and tell him in the presence of his loving wife and sunny-faced children he must be ready in ten minutes to go with you and then see the looks of sadness and despair . . . the sad and bitter good-bye . . . the longing glance at the place most dear to him on earth as he slowly moves out of sight—this is indeed a sad and unpleasant task."

In the light of later events one of the most remarkable Polk letters was that of May 12, 1863, in which he said: "I see no chance of the war to stop before March, 1865"—and of course Lee surrendered just ten days after Polk's deadline date.

In November, 1864, Colonel Polk was elected to the state legislature by a vote of his army comrades and fellow citizens in Anson County, and a December 3, 1864, memo reads: "Am tonight serenaded. Whole Regiment calls me out. Band discourses sweet music. Have good time."

So much for the war record of Colonel Polk. Far more important to the South was the service he later rendered as an ex-Confederate. This occurred when he came into national acclaim as an agricultural spokesman and orator in a then predominantly rural nation and preached everywhere the doctrine later effectively proclaimed by Theodore Roosevelt, namely, that both sections should honor equally the men of the North and the men of the South "who fought for the right as God gave them to see the right." In 1888-1892 men were so close to the bitternesses of war and Reconstruction it seems remarkable that Colonel Polk could so allay sectionalism that a multitude of men in the North and West who had worn the blue joined with a multitude in the South who had worn the gray in demanding "Polk For President" to

*head their newly organized agrarian party and thus lead
them out of the wilderness of hard times which had cursed
all agricultural America in the late 1880's and early 1890's.
(Incidentally this was the only time since the Civil War
when a majority of the members of any party have plainly
wanted a Southerner for President.)*

*Other interesting subjects in Colonel Polk's letters to his
wife are presented in greater detail as follows.*

Old Ford Church, Beaufort County, N.C., Oct. 31, 1862—
We are in a country, though one of the most fertile and
wealthy portions of the state, where we find it very difficult
to get supplies, the people having run off up the country
everything they could spare. They are for the most part
staunchly loyal, but considerably depressed by the annoy-
ing presence of the enemy and the inefficient protection they
have received from the government. It is nothing uncommon
for dozens of slaves to escape from one man in a day, or for
a plantation to be effectually ruined in a few hours. This
could easily be stopped by a small force of the right kind of
men.

Camp French, Dec. 24, 1862—One of the generals was
drunk during the fight on Wednesday and ordered a small
regiment [52nd] to charge a battery of eight pieces and
twenty times his number of men for one mile across an open
field, without any support in the face of a most murderous
fire. Of course they did not reach it. They had eight killed
and seventy-nine wounded in the charge. Another instance
of bad generalship is forcibly exhibited in the fact that one
single Yankee burned the railroad bridge before the faces of
two of our regiments.

The South Carolina troops under [name omitted] were
completely demoralized and the whole woods filled with
them. Their bad conduct no doubt is attributed to a great

degree to their rash and drunken leader. Our regiment was called upon to arrest and rally them. The coolness and composure of our men very soon restored order to the panic-stricken men. Our generals have great confidence in our regiment (too much to please me for we will always have the hard fighting to do and I fear will be greatly exposed).

Camp French, Dec. 24, 1862—The officers thought when our South Carolina friends were making such good speed that the county bridge one-fourth mile above the railroad was sure to fall in the hands of the Yankees. Accordingly General Smith sent us an order that we must retake it at the point of the bayonet. This order, which has no parallel case in the history of the world except Napoleon's storming of the bridges of Lodi and Arcola, was received with shouts and yells by the boys. Fortunately the order was premature, for it would have meant terrible slaughter.

We advanced in splendid order to our position behind the bank of the railroad and I had the pleasure of seeing the Yankee line of battle. It stretched out like some huge serpent uncoiling himself for a blow, and reaching for a mile across the level field of our front. Slowly, but in splendid order, it advanced with the stars and stripes floating in the breeze, which seemed to whisper that Death was again about to resume his feast of carnage. I could not help admiring the beautiful order and measured tread of the villains as they neared us. They approached within 500 yards of us, where they halted. Soon night dropped gently her sable curtain over the awful and solemnly silent scene. But thank God, they retreated.

I intend to send you money every time I can. Adjutant Jordan says he will take my boots at $35. He may have them if he will and as soon as I get it I will send the money to you to use, for I can draw a pair of shoes soon and . . . [they] will do for me.

I am not yet well of the itch. Dr. Warren is preparing me a very simple and pleasant remedy which will cure it very quick.

March 8, 1863—Well about that Negro marriage. I have never thought of it since my return until last week. I suppose we will have to agree to it, though if I had known it in time I would have stopped it. The first time there is a rumpus in the family I will break it up and I want you to tell them so.

March 25, 1863—I would like to write much more but my paper is out. I had to write a letter for another man to his wife to get this sheet. I got the pen from another, the ink from another, and a knapsack to write on from another and I am seated by a rotten pine log. So you can excuse this bad writing and the matter, too, when I assure you that about 100 boys are frolicking and playing "hot jacket" all around me.

April 11, 1863—We hear and see so much cannonading that we pay no attention to it. It is almost a constant thing. I have had a good time down on the river. We had no one to bother us and we could catch fine perch and cats. You ought to see me cooking them.

April 19, 1863—We went to a section where slave labor is gone—the people depending solely and entirely upon their own labor for support, and General Hill took almost every man able to do anything and sent them to the conscript camp. I took up thirty-eight and nearly all of their families (generally large) are almost entirely destitute of food and the means to produce it. But military power is inexorable and he swayed it with a merciless hand. The people believe that he could have captured Washington at first, but he stripped the country of men and provisions, laid waste their farms, and now returns with their curses upon him.

May 9, 1863—Wednesday we started to Cove Creek. That evening and night it rained—no, it poured down. I had nothing but my overcoat, neither did the Captain. We stayed in an old field. I lay down wet in the water and slept.

Next day we went to the creek and our company was detailed to go over near the Yankee camp after some women and children and baggage—refugees from Newbern the Yankees had brought out and emptied on the ground. They stayed out all night in the rain—had been there several days. We got what four wagons could bring and left the others to wait until we could hire some private wagons to send for them. There were seventy-nine of them and mostly women and children, wives of soldiers in our army.

We marched thirty-two miles that day and did not rest over one hour, and over half of it was through water from shoe to knee deep. We marched until one o'clock at night. I slept about two or three hours on the wet ground without anything to lie on or to cover with. I can wear out a good pair of socks in two days. If I had some boots I could do much better. . . . Our brigade has to shoot two deserters Monday.

June 28, 1863—You see that I am in Pennsylvania with the army that has so long threatened to "carry the war into Africa." We have destroyed millions of public property. Captured about 5,000 prisoners and are now encamped in and around the town of Carlisle. We all have just as much ice, sugar, molasses, beef, bread, etc., as we want. We are now occupying Yankee barracks. They are splendid quarters and comfortably furnished. The people are almost frightened to death and render a servile complacency to all our acts which it is painful to a bold Southerner to behold.

Aug. 6, 1863—Old Abe has issued an order saying that he will henceforth treat us just as we treat his Negro prisoners. If we put them to work he will put a like number of our men to work for the same length of time. If we kill any of them—he will kill, too.

Aug. 22, 1863—I wrote you about a boy and would like very much to have one, but at this season it would be quite a risk as they would be likely to get sick, but one of my Negroes is no better than I am. . . . You will have to keep Hark, and Wily will do more for you than Jerry, but the difficulty about Jerry is that he is not smart enough. I should want to send him home occasionally and I would not like to risk him, though he would be a great help to me. Think about it and you had better not send one until you gather your crop. . . . One thing is certain they will never more than make a support at home.

Sept. 10, 1863—There are seventy-six in my company now and we have three small vessels to cook in. They seldom get cool. There are not a dozen blankets in the company. Many of the men lie on leaves, three or four together, and cover with one blanket. It is hard, but these noble fellows cannot endorse the course of the thoughtless and misguided who think of a cowardly and ruinous submission.

Sept. 28, 1863—Their camp and pickets are very distinct from where I now sit. Our pickets and theirs exchange papers, talk, and seem to be more of neighbors than enemies. One of them told our boys yesterday that they were expecting a supply of winter clothing in a few days and that we ought not to fight them until it was received as we would be sure to get it all from them. Our boys cross the river in full sight of them and gather beans, peas, and corn.

Feb. 14, 1864—I find the prevailing opinion among financiers is that our currency by some contemplated action of Congress will soon be greatly enhanced in value. In fact Vice-President Stephens made a speech at Florence Tuesday night in which he advised the people to "hold on to their Confederate currency, that it would be worth something in two months." In view of this it probably would be well to sell what cotton you have on hand. Isaac could engage it to be delivered at sometime during spring or summer. . . .

Liquor plentiful at $35 per quart and truly consumed if we are to judge from its usual effects.

June 9, 1864—We have slept on the *same ground* three nights for the first time since April 14. I have not pulled off my clothes to sleep since that time and over half the time I sleep with boots on. The pants are threadbare and torn, drawers ditto. I have on the same suit and have worn no other—no change for two months. Where I find we will rest an hour or two, I do without my undersuit until I can wash it out. But there is one thing about it, I find myself in the tip of fashion with at least 10,000 Confederates for they are often worse off than myself. For an officer to be ragged and almost barefoot and dirty excites no remark.

July 17, 1864—We lived high in Maryland and I am persuaded that the people at the very gates of Washington are as *true as steel to the South.* . . . I captured four horses in the mountains on the seventh and since that time I have been mounted on a splendid horse. I will keep him some time and none but him who has followed this army through this campaign can properly appreciate the worth of a horse. . . .

July 25, 1864—We are living independently. Get beef from the Yanks, also wheat from the country and have it ground, but *go naked.* We get no money either. I do my own washing, patching, and will now have to do my own cooking.

Aug. 2, 1864—We are living very well and have on this whole trip with the exception of a few days. But dirty and ragged! You never saw the like. All laugh and frolic as though it were all right.

Aug. 8, 1864—I wish those Negroes were not so prolific. I know you are working yourself very hard. Take John in the house and if they can't make a support let them live without it.

Sept. 11, 1864—Since April 18 [the fight at Plymouth] we have marched 1300 or 1400 miles. Have been in eight or ten battles besides skirmishes. Have lost 315 men, 67 were killed. We are marching and countermarching all the time nearly. We get plenty to eat, but are nearly all naked. I expect we have fifty barefoot men in the Regiment. . . . I understand that owing to some petty difference between the President of the Central Railroad and Postmaster General letters are not conveyed on that road unless the postage is prepaid. So now I am perplexed to know whether you ever got any of my letters for I have not had a stamp in months and it is impossible to get any.

Oct. 19, 1864—I should like also to make some arrangements to get rid of our surplus Negroes for next year. They don't pay us.

CHAPTER FIVE

War When Soldiers Were Not Fighting

SO MUCH HAS BEEN TOLD AND WRITTEN ABOUT SOLDIERS IN *combat that to the average young person a soldier is somebody who is always fighting or preparing to fight next day. Actually, of course, no soldier was ever fighting most of the time. The hours, days, and months when Civil War soldiers were not in battle offered many opportunities for relaxation, humor, romance, and fraternizing.*

One of the most vital concerns of a soldier at leisure has always been food. Especially was this true of the Confederate who rarely had all he wanted. Hunger was a deciding factor in many battles, Vicksburg for instance, where the Federals knew that if they waited long enough the Southerners would have to surrender—or starve.

Dr. J. Richard Corbett writes:

Both Federals and Confederates craved "fresh" meat; and both engaged in killing cows and hogs belonging to civilians and distributing the meat among their troops. During the final months of the war, more than a few horses, mules, dogs, cats, and even rats were eaten by soldiers, particularly prisoners of war.

In the closing months of 1863, the 18th North Carolina Regiment marched to Mine Run, built breastworks, and lay in line of battle opposite a Yankee regiment. Between the lines in a thicket of old field pines, a flock of wild turkeys lit down. The advent of these birds served to unite the opposing forces under a single objective, namely, to get some fresh meat. As a result a fine large gobbler lost his life. Each side determined to capture that turkey; and once again the rifles were turned on each other. The spirit of competition intensified the appetite for fresh meat. After sundown George W. Corbett, my great grandfather, planned a lateral approach to the target. Maneuvering slowly along the ground, weaving in and out between the trees and sliding beneath the underbrush, he succeeded in bagging the game—plus a new overcoat and blanket off an equally venturesome, but less successful, blue-coater who lay nearby. The pot boiled that night among the North Carolina ranks.

Another story involving an animal caught between the lines is told by Henry P. Rudasill of Catawba County, North Carolina:

The next morning [at Fredericksburg] about eight o'clock, a red fox was discovered between the picket lines of the two armies, which occasioned much amusement on both sides. We had strict orders not to fire unless the enemy advanced upon us; but Reynard offered a temptation we could not resist. Fired upon by our pickets, the fox ran first in the direction of the Yankees, and when fired upon by them rushed back toward us—and so on, back and forth, down the line for about three miles. Whether the fox was killed I do not know.

The Negro cooks who served the Confederate soldiers on the battlefield also felt the pinch of lack of food as is shown in this story told by J. M. Cutchin in a history he wrote of his life as a soldier:

The Rev. Jesse H. Page ... was chaplain of the regiment and ate at our table and had an old Negro cook by the name of Willis Cutchen. Coffee, sure enough coffee, was a rare thing with us, but old Willis, somehow and somewhere, got us a little good coffee. We did not bother about how he got it, but Mr. Page, in saying grace that night, accidentally knocked over one of Willis's cups of coffee, when old Willis cried out, "La, Mr. Page, I wouldn't a-give that cup of coffee for *three* graces,"—and nobody laughed more than the parson.

More often than not, however, the scarcity of food was no laughing matter as is illustrated in this portrait of weary soldiers returning from battle. This reminiscence was handed down to Mr. Rance J. McLeroy of Natchitoches, Louisiana, by his grandmother, Mrs. Mary Higgenbotham, and he writes: "Sixty years after that memorable Saturday afternoon, I have seen big hot tears come down Grandma's cheeks as she told of this incident:"

'Twas now Saturday afternoon of April [1864] and we heard the roar of cannon at Mansfield the afternoon before and received rumors that a desperate battle had been fought. We knew not whether we'd see the Yankee army or our army before the day was over. Then about 1:30 we heard the low rumble of drums in the direction of Grove Hill and in a few minutes the sound of marching feet. The children ran to the house from the bend of the road excitedly telling us, "There they come—there come the soldiers!" Just as they told us we saw a column of ragged, weary, gray-clad men marching in columns of fours, coming around the bend of the road. Walker's Texas Infantry Brigade had fought at Moss' Lane and the Bridwell place the afternoon before. They halted in front of our house, then stacked arms in the road and were told to "fall out" for a fifteen minute rest.

Some had blood-stained bandages on their heads—some had an arm suspended in a bloody bandage or wore bandages on their necks or shoulders. Many of them fell prostrate on the ground, too exhausted to move. Others staggered toward the house to beg for a bite to eat. The yard and house were soon full of the tired and haggard men—some with the most haunted look in their eyes I have ever seen. She (my mother) gave them all the leftovers from dinner (in fact we had been too excited to eat any dinner at all) but still they kept begging, "Mom, save some for me. I haven't had a bite since Thursday evening. Please, just one bite." Next Ma went out to the backyard followed by dozens of ragged, bearded men. Our big old washpot (probably a hundred years old) was full of freshly cooked lye hominy, warm and ready to eat. So she began issuing it out with a large wooden cooking spoonful to each man. Some of them took it in the crown of their dirty hats, some in their bare, dirty hands, some in cups or on pieces of boards they had picked up. All of them ate it right there like a pack of hungry wolves.

When the hominy was gone she next went to the smokehouse, which contained the family's meager supply of bacon for the coming months. There she began cutting up sides of bacon into portions half as large as your hand, handing a piece to each man as with tears in their eyes they begged for it. An officer on horseback at the road sent his orderly to the house to beg for a piece of bacon for him and the man begged Ma to "please give him some bacon for his Captain." Before the man reached the gate on his way back with the precious morsel the officer galloped up to the fence and was leaning far over into the yard when the orderly reached him. The look of hunger and despair in his face and eyes was something that has haunted me ever since that day. Grabbing the piece of meat he tore into it with his teeth at once.

Soon the smokehouse as well as the washpot was empty. But the men seemed reluctant to leave, crowding around Ma to thank her again and again and to invoke the blessings of Heaven upon her. Some handed her a dollar bill, some two dollars or even five (Confederate money) and others hugged her as they left the yard. They had marched all night Thursday night, marched and fought all day Friday, then buried their dead at Moss' Lane during that night—all with only a few hours sleep and without a bite to eat since Thursday.

A blast of the bugle soon brought the men back to the road where they secured their rifles and quickly lined up. Then the order rang out sharp and clear, "Attention! F-o-h-r-w-a-r-d—M-a-h-r-c-h!" Then the order, "Double quick!—M-a-h-r-c-h!" Soon they disappeared in a cloud of dust in the direction of Pleasant Hill.

For some of the more fortunate soldiers there were quite pleasant ways of passing time while waiting for the war to resume. One of the most profitable, if not popular, pastimes was humorously described in The Falling Flag:

... We were waiting for orders by our fire, and filled up the time pressing [confiscating] horses in the town, from a kind consideration of the owners, that they should not fall into the hands of the Yankees. ...

... One of our young lieutenants had heard of a very fine bay stallion, belonging to a gentleman in town, and as the rumor had spread that pressing horse flesh was going on, he went off promptly with a man or two, reached the house, and was met at the door by a young and pretty woman, who, with all the elegant kindness of a Virginia lady, asked him to come in. He felt doubtful, but could not resist, ordering his men to hold on a minute or two while he talked horse with the lady, wishing, in the innocent kindness of his heart, to break it to her gently. After a few minutes' general conversation he touched on the horse question. "Oh! yes, sir," she said, getting up and looking through a window that overlooked the back yard. "Yes, sir; I am sorry to disappoint you, but as you came in at the front door my husband was saddling the bay, and while you were talking to me I saw him riding out of the back gate. I am so sorry: *indeed I am.*" With a hasty good morning our lieutenant rode back to camp upon a horse some degrees below the standard of a "Red Eye" or any other race horse. The laugh was with the lady!

Evidently it was hard for soldiers at leisure to sit around hating the enemy. Instead they often thought up ways of enjoying each other, as reported in two letters from Catawba County, North Carolina, Confederates. Says George W. Rabb: "On the Rappahannock, the river being the dividing line between the armies, we made this mutual agreement—not to fire at each other, unless giving due notice. We thus became right familiar for enemies, and one day they asked us to come over that night and have a game of seven up. We did so, and while we were intensely engaged in a game, the relief came around and demanded our surrender. The old guard said, 'No, we invited them over, and promised protection, and we mean to see the Johnnies back in safety,' and so they did."

And this report came from P. A. Hoyle: "During our stay

here, we did guard duty along the river with our enemy in full view on the other side. We frequently would converse and exchange products with our blue-coated fellow guards. A field of nice corn lay between the lines and agreements were entered into that pretty nearly divided the corn between the two governments. . . . A flock of sheep was ranging between the lines of the sharp-shooters and after some private negotiations, small parts of both armies enjoyed mutton chops."

And a Texas soldier wrote to his son:

I embrace the present Sabbath in writing to you. . . . I am on picket guard in sight of the enemy pickets. In some places on our picket line we run very close together but the pickets do not fire at each other. And sometimes some of the pickets meet at the creek between us and exchange papers and sometimes trade with each other. When they want to swap papers they hold up their papers and then meet and swap and that gives them a chance to trade. Our men trade tobacco for coffee and knives or anything they have to trade for. And I expect this will seem strange to you but it is the case, but they have to be sly about it for it is strictly against orders. The enemy sometimes throws a shell or two at our pickets from a battery they have and make the boys skedaddle and did kill a man the other day. . . .

The distinguished Henry Wallace of Iowa told of similar conditions existing when he, as a mounted Federal army chaplain, was near Richmond not long before Lee's surrender: "On a clear day," Wallace wrote, "we could see the church spires of Richmond. The swapping of tobacco and provisions was constantly going on between the breastworks of both armies, only a short distance apart." And he then added this remarkable sentence: "Desertions from the Con-

federates were frequent and desertions to the Confederates almost as frequent."

When not actually fighting, soldiers of course spent much time thinking about home, longing to see their loved ones, worrying about how things were on the farm or plantation, and writing letters. In a letter from Mrs. Craige Jones of North Carolina is a vivid description of the homesickness of one soldier facing a Christmas away from home: "We are going to have a glorious time Christmas. I expect to get up before sunrise off my pallet of straw (wish I was home), eat some beef and biscuit (wish I was home), take a smoke out of my cob pipe, and wish I was at home again—and so on throughout the day."

Another letter sent by Mrs. Hugh Warren, Sr., of Mississippi describes the discouragement of some Southerners with their cause when intervals between battles gave them time to think about it. This letter written May 8, 1864, is significant in that it reveals the demoralizing effect upon soldiers resulting from the law passed by the Confederate Congress exempting from military service persons with twenty or more working slaves.

In view of the fact of the scarcity of subsistence in the South, we are now amid our greatest peril and upon the eve of great events. We will have to have almost miraculous successes and follow them up closely even to get upon terms of equality with the enemy. We have already lost all our own subsistence country in the South and a large refugee population thrown back on the Atlantic states that never made a subsistence in time of peace. The substitute and exemption laws, making distinction between the rich and the poor, have also demoralized the army and people to an alarming extent.

In view of all these facts, I think the ultimate success of our cause extremely doubtful. There is a principle gaining ground here, to wit: that we compromise for our independence by acceding to a gradual emancipation of negroes for fifty or seventy-five years which I think under all circumstances will be the best arrangement we could make. I think the time has arrived for a final settlement of the slave question. At least it is better than a fevered or precipitate emancipation without time or preparation. There is already discernible a large emancipation element existing in the northern portion of the South which at some future time would embroil us in another Civil War—the greatest misfortune that can befall a country.

The most painful inactivity forced upon soldiers came when they were wounded. Mrs. R. L. Simpson of Texas sent this moving narrative from her family history of a young soldier's courage—and his later determination to go home.

Adam Clements was mustered into service in the Confederate Army early in the Civil War. In the latter part of the last year of the war he was severely wounded at the battle of Jenkins Ferry in Louisiana. . . .

The next day two army surgeons examined his wound. They told him the leg would have to be amputated. Adam protested vehemently. But the surgeons told him if the leg was not amputated he would die. "Then I will die with the leg on my body," he said. The doctors paid no attention to his protest and soon came with their surgical instruments and a nurse to perform the operation.

Adam had a dirk knife under his pillow which he had carried with him for many years. When the surgeons came near, Adam drew the knife and said, "I'll kill the first man that attempts to cut my leg off." The surgeons left him to die.

The next day a young doctor who was attending patients discovered Adam in a precarious condition. This Doctor Harrison remarked, "This man has been neglected." The doctor cleansed the wound, extracted the bullet and fragments of bone, then brought the two ends of the bone together, making the leg five inches shorter than the other. After that Adam lingered between life and death for six weeks before beginning to convalesce. Later he was given a crutch which enabled him to hobble around in the building.

Adam told some friends that he believed if he had a gentle horse and a saddle he could ride a few miles each day on the journey to his father's home in Bell County—450 miles away. His friends procured the horse and saddle, helped him to mount the steed, and watched him ride slowly away with his crutch in front of him across the saddle.

It certainly required superhuman courage to tackle that long trip alone in his weakened condition. He felt he would encounter hunger and thirst because he could not dismount or remount his horse without aid. He was dependent upon the kindness of settlers along the road for food and lodging at nights. But he found kindness all the way and never suffered for want of aid.

In about thirty days Adam appeared in front of his father's home. When he was discovered sitting on a horse with a crutch in front of him, a cry went out from several voices, "Adam! Adam! The dead has come to life."

Next we hear directly from one of the most gifted and perceptive writers who themselves saw hospitals at first hand. Such a man was Major Charles H. Smith of Georgia, long known as "Bill Arp." Along with all his other qualities which made him the most popular weekly columnist in the Southern press, Bill Arp had the same saving sense of humor which enabled so many of his comrades to survive all the

*years of bloodshed. "If this was a civil war," he asserted, "I
hope never to fight in an uncivil one!" And as for his marks-
manship, he said, "I killed as many of them as they did of
me." In the account which follows, however, there was no
opportunity for humor:*

I remember a very graphic scene that I witnessed on the
night after the first battle of Manassas.

The hospital chosen was a large brick building near the
battleground. It was property that had been vacated under
military orders. But the surgeons' operating-room was not
there. It was in a willow glade not far away, where there was
a clear spring branch flowing peacefully along. Dr. Miller
ordered all the wounded brought there, for the night was
beautiful and the water convenient.

All night long he and his assistants amputated arms and
legs, probed for balls, and used bandages and splints and
other appliances, and as fast as one man was fixed up he
was taken away and the doctor said, "Next," like a barber in
a barber shop. But there was no groaning. The boys were
heroes under the surgeon's knife as well as in the battlefield.

I remember when Jett Howard, of Kingston, limped up
without assistance, and the doctor said:

"What's the matter with you, Jett?"

Jett pointed to where a Minié ball had penetrated his hip,
and said he could feel it on the other side. Quickly the doctor thrust a probe into the wound and as quickly drew it out,
and turning Jett around and sounding for the ball under
the skin, he found it. With his knife he cut an opening and
thrusting in his finger pulled out the ball and gave it to him.
"Here's your diploma, Jett," he said. "Next."

Jett limped away with a smile and had his wounds dressed.
When my brother-in-law, Captain Cooper, was brought up
with a shattered leg, his kneepan crushed and his bones

mangled, the doctor said: "Fred, this leg must come off immediately," and he reached for his knife and his saw, "Stop, doctor," exclaimed Fred, "can't you save my leg?" "No, it is impossible," said he. "It must come off, I tell you." "Doctor, is there a possible chance for me to save this leg?" "Perhaps," said the doctor, "one chance in a hundred; but I warn you now, that if it is not speedily cut off you will be a dead man within two weeks." Captain Cooper was full of nerve and faith. "Doctor, I will take the chance," he said, and the doctor said, "Next."

Fred was taken to the hospital that night and died in two weeks.

Bill Arp also witnessed the results of battle fatigue. Here is one of his most unforgettable experiences:

On the sixth day of the Chickahominy fight, when McClellan was in full retreat, our brigade commander, General Anderson, sent me down to the river to General Lee's headquarters for some instructions about moving the brigade. I found him in a large wall tent with many officers around him. This tent opened into another where the camp tables were set for dinner and the servant was bringing it in. There were four or five large camp tables joined together, and as I sat upon my horse waiting for a reply I saw a man, an officer, whose head and body were under the right hand table and his feet out upon the straw. His slouched hat was over the head and eyes; his sword was not unbuckled, and his boots were on and spurred. His Confederate gray clothes seemed faded and worn.

My curiosity was greatly excited, and when the adjutant handed me the instructions I ventured to point to the sleeping man and to ask, "Who is that?"

"That is Stonewall," he said. "He has had no sleep for forty-eight hours, and fell down there exhausted. General Lee would not suffer him to be disturbed, and so our dinner will be eaten over him and in silence."

Reverently I gazed upon him for a minute, for I felt almost like I was in the presence of some divinity. . . .

CHAPTER SIX

Diary of a Soldier's Wife
on Looking Glass Plantation

ONE OF THE MOST ARTICULATE DIARISTS OF THE CIVIL WAR PE-
riod was Catherine Deveraux Edmondston. The following
excerpts from her diary (part of which was edited by Margaret Mackay Jones and privately printed by Mrs. Stephen H.
Millender) are concerned mostly with her life on Looking
Glass Plantation in Halifax County, North Carolina. While
visiting in Charleston in 1861 Mrs. Edmondston saw Fort Sumter fired on and heard an amazing story of Southern chivalry
to the enemy. With a real shock, a day or two later, she read in
a Charleston newspaper dispatches from Washington headed
"Foreign News." She felt the ominous impact of war even
more vividly when her husband gave her a pistol. But while
Mrs. Edmondston observed many tragedies of war, she welcomed its touches of humor—as when a lively Southern lady
deposited an abandoned Negro baby on a Yankee general's
desk. Born in 1823 in Raleigh, North Carolina, her diary indicates that she was well educated, cultured, and refined. In
1846 she married Patrick Edmondston, of a wealthy, aristo-
cratic Charleston family and they came to live at Looking
Glass Plantation. The following excerpts from her diary be-

gin in September, 1860, so the reader may get a glimpse of the life and attitudes before the coming of what she calls "this needless, cruel war."

September 5, 1860—Bessie and James left after a fortnight's visit which we enjoyed greatly. James gives us gloomy news of the antagonistic temper of the North: Abolitionism rampant! . . . I cannot believe that we will ever have such a man as Abraham Lincoln President of the U.S. No! It cannot be—though Patrick says it will!

October 6—Father, Mama, and Sue arrived from the Virginia Springs—all in good health and spirits. Father is sure of Bell's election and oh! how he abuses that fellow Douglas. I for my part think Douglas as bad as Lincoln and I believe he will do just as much as Lincoln to undermine the South and slavery! This wretched Missouri Compromise! I cannot see why Clay ever made it!

November 6—Election day. No fears in my mind that Lincoln will be elected though Patrick feels gloomy about it. Brother John is enough to depress anyone; he talks so gloomily about debts, politics, etc. *Ruin* is a household word with him. If we are to die, let it be but once—not daily! As to politics Peter is worse than brother. He thinks us on the eve of civil war. Father hoots at it and abuses South Carolina for her ultra views and particularly for sending commissioners to Virginia after the John Brown Raid last fall to consult about a uniform policy for the South. I dread to hear him!

November 25—I left off on election day when I would not be persuaded that Lincoln would be elected—but how grievously I was disappointed. The South was divided between Bell, Breckenridge and Douglas. Would that we, as a people, had studied Aesop to better advantage. On the 18th we went to Raleigh, finding all well and as happy as possible, though brother is dreadfully gloomy about the future. It is disagreeable to be with Mr. Miller, and Sister Frances is no better. She says "You slave holders have lived so long on your plantations with no one to gainsay or contradict you, and the Negroes only looking up to and worshipping you, that you expect to govern everybody, and have it all your own way. I can see it in Father—in Brother John—in Brother Patrick—and in you, too." Truly a pleasant way to spend the half hour before dinner. But let it pass. I do not think that every one estimates the price of words—words are things. She does not realize that she is calling her kinsmen domineering, arbitrary and insolent—but so she is.

December 8—Patrick out with his troop all day, I hard at work icing a marshmallow cake which I intend to carry to Papa and Mama for their anniversary—their golden wedding on the 25th of December. Fifty years married! Think of it! But to my cake—it has some of all the good things I got from New York in it—as rich as all my cookbooks can make it! But the icing is the point on which I rest my fame! Pure white . . . on the top Papa's and Mama's monogram CME surrounded with the words "25th Dec 1810" done in pure white couplets—then beading of white sugar plums, festoons, etc., on the side of the first tier. The second is divided by sugar plums into eleven medallions, each medallion containing the initials of one of their children.

December 12—This teaching of Negroes is a sore problem to me! It ought to be done and I ought to do it. I am afraid I magnify the lions in the path because it is disagreeable. They learn nothing from me but the mere rudiments of Christianity—who made them, who redeemed them, with the certainty of a future reward or punishment, the Creed, the Ten Commandments—and exhortations against lying and stealing—and only the little ones get that. My difficulties I am convinced beset many a well-intentioned mistress who, like me, does nothing because she cannot do what she feels she *ought*.

December 17—Left Raleigh on the 21st via Wilmington having changed our route on account of smallpox prevailing in Columbia. The Convention has also adjourned to Charleston. On the 22nd between Wilmington and Florence met Dr. Tennant and Mr. Greff who told us of the secession of South Carolina—the Ordinance was signed upon the 20th of December. So South Carolina is no longer one of the United States! One link is missing! One pearl lost from the glorious string! Pray God that it be not the beginning of evils as Patrick predicts!

December 25—On the 25th their fiftieth wedding day—we had everything arranged for a series of surprises to our dear old people. Besides presents from their children many of their friends and persons whom Papa had befriended took the opportunity of testifying their gratitude or affection. Before they were out in the morning the drawing room carpet was taken up and replaced by a new one sent by Mr. Whilden of Charleston. . . . Then a pair of arm chairs Patrick and I ordered from New York and whose ponderous box had exercised Papa's curiosity the day before. On the breakfast table were new cups from Charles' children, a silver egg stand from James, spoons, salt cellars, butter dishes, and in short I cannot enumerate everything. Then a table was laid out in her chamber holding the bridal gifts. New toilet appurtenances such as Mama delights in, caps, elegant lace collars and sleeves, vases, china, ornaments, slippers, cologne, trifles from the grandchildren, an elegant bouquet containing a white camellia, embroidered handkerchiefs, stockings—more than they could possibly want or use. Indeed Papa frequently said it was the happiest day of his life! We all treated and addressed Mama as a bride. . . . In the afternoon we were all busy in laying out the supper and an elegant and bountiful one it was. We sorted out all the relics of Mama's former grandeur—the elegant buff china, the glass, and the table fairly groaned with her silver. . . . In the center was my cake and very much delighted was my dear Papa with both the design and execution. He was never weary of admiring it and was much opposed to cutting it.

Then at night when all was ready we put on our best apparel and assembled in the drawing room. Papa entered dressed in a suit of clothes woven for this very occasion—in his own native land—of his own Shetland wool. Mama was elegantly dressed in a rich brocaded black silk dress and lace cap, collar, and sleeves to match. The clergyman, Mr. Cornish, made a handsome and appropriate address, altering the marriage ceremony, making the ring an evidence of past happiness and a pledge for future—then a prayer—and congratulations and felicitations from all the children and grandchildren. Then came an old fashioned *contredanse* headed by Papa and Mama, Mrs. Matheson and Lawrence—and filled up in regular gradation with sons and their wives, daughters and their husbands—and grandchildren down to Jessie's youngest—a little two-year old! It was astonishing to see how Mama danced . . . how she took her steps and enjoyed it! Papa danced a Highland Fling with Isabella to the tune of the Fisher's Housewife. He had a Scotch bonnet on his head and he took the steps as well as a man of thirty could have—throwing out his legs from the knees as the Horn Pipe ought to be danced but rarely is, and snapping his fingers at the right moment in unison with the music.

Then came supper. Papa gave health after health, toast after toast, calling on each member of the family to respond which they all did in the happiest manner. At last came the crowning act—the cutting of the cake. Then worn out with happiness the dear old lady and gentleman retired, Papa repeating that it was the happiest day of his life! Long may they be spared, the centre and head of a united family.

December 27—The ladies of South Carolina displayed an enthusiasm and earnestness in their preparations for war that was almost sublime in its unity and self-devotion. They spent their whole time scraping lint, making bandages. One lady in Aiken made 500 with her own hands. . . . South Carolina having seceded from the U. S.—amidst the jeers and laughter of the whole country—calmly organized her own government and prepared for war singly and alone. It at first made one smile to see the news from Washington put under the head of "Foreign News." I often thought, "Have we indeed come to this!"

January 9, 1861—On the Seventh of January we left Aiken for Charleston taking little Frank Coffin with us. On the morning of the ninth as we were dressing we suddenly heard the report of a heavy gun followed by another and another! A few moments sufficed to collect us all out in front of the house where we had a fine view of Sumter, Moultrie, and the channel. And there, sad to relate, steaming up the channel was a vessel with the U.S. flag flying at her peak! The expected reinforcements for Sumter doubtless! Boom! another cannon from the shore batteries on Morris Island. Is she struck? No, on she comes. Another and another! whilst Sumter opens her portholes and slowly runs out her cannon prepared for instant action. Now a heavy gun from Fort Moultrie. Will Sumter respond? No, not yet. Another from Moultrie. How with Sumter now? Silent! The vessel turns slowly. Is she struck? No one can tell. But slowly, reluctantly as it were, almost with a baffled look, the steamer retreats down the channel. Thank God, every one ejaculates! . . . Eleven guns in all were fired. Good God! Is this the beginning of the Civil War of which we have heard so much?

Sister Frances is a terrible Unionist. Right or wrong this
"Glorious Union" is everything. When it ceases to be voluntary it degenerates into a hideous oppression. I mourn over
it as for a lost friend, but do not seek to enforce it. President
Buchannon [*sic*] could do much now, but does nothing.
"Apres nous le Deluge" is his motto. During this past month
Florida, Louisiana, Mississippi, Georgia, and Alabama have
all passed ordinances of secession. The first of this month
Texas also went out. The Southern states I see take the name
of Confederate States, and have assembled in Montgomery
to form a provisional government. This humbug of a Peace
Convention now assembled in Washington will do nothing.
It is not equal to the emergencies of the times!

Planted fruit trees in the front yard.

January 16—Sister Frances left. I have not enjoyed her
visit as I should have done were she less violent and bitter.
She thinks we should let the "few Negroes go," but it is not
just a "few Negroes," it is the country—for I should like to
know who could live here if they were freed? Then the
principle! I yield nothing where my *Liberty*—my *Honour*—
dearer than life, are concerned. She knows no more about
the proper management of Negroes than a child, tho she
has had them under her since she came to woman's estate.
She thinks all discipline severity—yet complains if they are
not perfect, and makes them ten times more unhappy by her
want of government—than severe masters do by their excess
of it.

January 18—Today was inaugurated at Montgomery—Jefferson Davis, President of the Confederate States of America. O, that North Carolina would join her Southern sisters.
Virginia is jealous because she—"The Mother of States," did
not lead the movement. She will be the jag end of the "Dis-
united States" ere long.

It gets almost painful to go to Father's, we differ so widely.

That hateful "National Intelligencer" is a fruitful bone of contention. A vile, unjust, deceitful sheet, yet at Father's it is a text book—a political Koran.

March 4—Today was inaugurated that wretch, Abraham Lincoln, President of the U. S. We are told not to speak evil of dignities—but it is hard to realize that he is a dignity. Ah, would that Jefferson Davis were our President. He is a man to whom a gentleman could look, without mortification, as chief of the nation. Well—we have a rail splitter and a tall man at the head of our affairs!

March 5—Mr. E. and I set out fruit trees. Patrick is dreadfully despondent and enough to take the heart out of one. Whilst we were planting a tree—I holding it and he throwing in the earth, he suddenly stopped—and said "Where is the use? . . . depend on it, before this tree bears fruit we shall be in the midst of the most desperate war this world has ever seen." Pray God he prove a false prophet.

March 6—At Father's. Could I have believed that any Southern person could have liked Lincoln's message? But so it is,—Mama and Susan both. Father does not like it and looks gloomy indeed.

March 19—[Back at home.] Had an amusing illustration of the value in which Cuffee [her word for slave] holds himself today. A little Negro boy, Sharper, and Frank [the young relative visiting the Edmondstons] were playing in the lot when little George came up with the sheep. Sharper began to banter him about his size and among other things wound up the climax by telling him he "warn't worth a hundred dollars!" "How much are you worth?" said Frank. "Me? I'm worth 500 dollars!" Frank, not wishing to be outdone, said, "How much am I worth?" "Lord, Marse Frank," said Sharper in a tone of disdain, "you's white. You ain't worth nothing!"

March 27—Mr. E. drilling his troops. Dined at Father's. Mama and Susan more enthusiastic over the "Flag" than ever. "The Flag under which we gained our liberties"—no such thing—it was adopted after, or about the time of the War of 1812.

April 15—Got full accounts of the bombardment of Sumter. The authorities of South Carolina having information that the fleet in N. Y. was ready to leave for the reinforcement of Sumter, they telegraphed to Montgomery and received positive instructions from the War Department to attack it. Accordingly on the morning of the twelfth very early the cannonading began. Sumter was silent until after breakfast when she responded east and west to Moultrie, the floating battery, and the batteries on Morris Island. Steadily the bombardment continued all day and all night without a casualty on either side. On Saturday the U.S. fleet with the expected reinforcements arrived off the harbour. Then the firing redoubled! Sumter signaled violently to her friends for aid—fought with her colours at half mast! Yet no aid came! Her flag is down! Has she surrendered? No, shot down by one of the batteries. Again she signals for assistance. Shame on the dastard Navy outside! So wore on the day. One chivalrous act I must mention. When the flag was shot down amidst the thickest of the fight, through the smoke of battle went a little boat with another U.S. flag for their enemy to fight under! Was ever anything handsomer?

April 16—Heard last night that Lincoln had issued his proclamation calling for 75,000 troops to compel South Carolina to obedience. [He] sent to the Governor of N.C. for [blank], that being the quota required of North Carolina. Thank God we had a governor who had spirit to refuse! Think of the insult the man puts on us, calling upon us to subdue our sister.

Never was known such excitement as was caused by Mr. Lincoln's proclamation. The whole South flew to arms.

April 20—Resume my journal which I fortunately find has

not all been destroyed. Went to Father's and found everyone
in intense excitement about the news of yesterday [the fighting in Baltimore]. Had not seen Mama since the fall of
Sumter, and almost dreaded to meet her. Mr. Edmondston
feels so keenly about it—his own flesh and blood having been
concerned in it—actually under fire—that I fear neither of
us will bear as patiently as perhaps we ought, the strictures
on South Carolina! . . . This difference of opinion with Father
has been very sad to me, for I think I can honestly say that
it is the first time in my life that my judgment and feelings
did not yield to him.

April 24—Frank and I went to Hascosea on a gardening
expedition. How lonely it is without Mr. E.—gardening is
no longer the same occupation. As I worked, Mrs. Heman's
lines "Bring flowers to strew in the conqueror's path" re-
curred to me again and again,—Yes, I will plant flowers for
the conqueror's path—for our own path! A short time of
conflict and the day is ours—ours for freedom—they can
never overcome us, for we fight for our birthright. Let them
try their boasted *Blockade!*—who cares! Who will be hurt
most—us? themselves? or England? Not us, for we make the
necessities of life—but what will England do for cotton—
when her looms are idle? King Cotton will raise his own
blockade in his own time in spite of Yankee vessels.

May 1—Hard at work all day cutting fatigue jackets. Had
the women [Negroes] at work in the piazza—and through
the open window could hear their comments on the war—
and the "cloth house" they were making for their master to
sleep under! "Yankees!" said one. "What are Yankees, sister?"
"Yankees . . . why that's them rampaging folks that come
a-cussin' and a-swearin' to Mount Roe! . . . like they was
gwine to take the plantation!"

May 2—Mr. Benton came in and read poetry to us all the
afternoon [while we sewed]. God help me! here I am sewing

on uniforms which may ere long be drenched in blood, the blood of my neighbors! Yes, perhaps of my own husband, and yet I am petty enough to be provoked at this well-meant but ill-timed poetry. Away with it! It no longer interests me. The time for it is past. I feel as though I could *live* poetry—poetry of the sternest and most heroic cast!

May 3—Brought home yesterday another tent on which my forces are busily engaged. The cloth for these uniforms and tents is purchased by individual subscription—not waiting for the state to equip its men—and this thing is going on all over the whole South! Thousands of ladies who never worked before are hard at work on coarse sewing all over our whole country.

May 17—Every day I have paid a visit to Patrick in camp. Unsatisfactory and tantalizing they are, but I prize them. Where he will be ordered none can tell, but wherever it may be—may I have the strength to cheerfully bid him go. I would not have him stay, when he can strike one blow for our freedom—our Native Land. Tomorrow he comes out of camp and will be a short time at home with me. Diamond dust will the moments be.

During the past week the threat of a blockade has been put into execution. Charleston, Norfolk, and New Orleans all have a fleet of war vessels off their harbours.

May 21—Preserved a large quantity of strawberries. Sugar will be scarce, but Patrick likes them. Found the stores which Patrick had ordered in anticipation of the blockade had arrived—salt—iron—cotton bagging—rope—coffee—sugar —and I know not what else. Enough to last for some months. Before fall the blockade must be raised. England and the U. S. cannot do without our cotton. Once let us have a supply and say to England "Come and get it," and the navies of Mr. Lincoln will be swept away like dust!

May 22—Heard today that on the twentieth it being the

anniversary of the signature of the Mecklenburg Declaration of Independence, the Convention of N. C. signed the Ordinance of Secession. The scene is said to have beggared description! Ramseur's battery stationed outside fired a salute of a hundred guns! This seemed a signal for men, women and children to flock to the State House. Everybody congratulated everybody else! Persons who had not spoken for years exchanged the most cordial and fraternal greeting.

June 1—When Patrick went into camp he sent me a present—his last—a Colt pistol. Now he is teaching me to use it. I was much struck by a remark Mr. E. made the other day. He said were he "Autocrat" he could put a stop to the war and restore peace to the land by *one single order.* "Certainly," said I, "You would order everybody, everywhere to lay down their arms and go home." No," he said, "I would stop *all* newspapers. This war is now fed and fanned by newspapers. They have lighted the fire, but they cannot control the conflagration."

July 8—I remember one of Dolly's attempts at consolation which in its simplicity and faith evinced such childlike confidence in her master, and such contempt for his enemies that I must record it. "Never mind, Mistress," she said, "Never mind,—Marster will not be gone long now, for them folks won't have the impudence to stand up—now that Marster himself has gone out agin' 'em."

September—One thing struck me throughout the whole progress of the summer; the universality—and the eagerness with which the women entered into the struggle! They work —as many of them had never worked before steadily and faithfully to supply the soldiers with clothing and the hospitals with comforts of various kinds—everything must be given to them and everything must be done for them.

November—On the eighteenth Patrick went up to Halifax Court and I well remember I took that day for digging up my dahlia roots—which had bloomed splendidly—and had been a great source of pleasure to me—but I had not been called to "strew them in the Conqueror's path"—nor to "deck the halls where the bright wine flows" in honour of peace as I had fondly thought when I planted them.

When Mr. E. came back he brought the news that our commissioners to France and England had been forcibly taken from the deck of an English steamer by an armed U.S. vessel. Ambassadors were pronounced "contraband"—their favorite word when they wanted anything. All eyes were bent on the foreign news to see what England would do or say, and the sentiment was universal that Mason and Slidwell [*sic*] in Fort Warren were doing more for their country than they would do—were they accredited at the Courts of St. James and St. Cloud.

December—On demand of the British for the captured commissioners, the government meekly gave up, and they were surrendered on the 26th of December. So closed the year for us. Disappointed in our hope for foreign aid, the coast of South Carolina ravaged, destroyed—Savannah threatened—Charleston in ashes—an immense fleet of mortar and gun boats preparing to descend the Mississippi—another army ready to march through Kentucky—Norfolk beleaguered, and blockaded—Fortress Monroe in the hands of our enemies—an army equal to our own facing us on the Potomac—another armada being fitted out for the coast of North Carolina—whilst preparations were actively making for the bombardment of New Orleans—the hearts of our people might well "fail—for fear," but they did not. Men and women looked the alternative sternly in the face, and preferred death!

February 10, 1862—Mr. Edmondston was off this morning. Before he left he had the Negroes summoned and told them of the enemy below and gave them orders that when the plantation bell should ring and the horn blow at the same time every one of them should assemble in the lot and accompany me to Hascosea [the Edmondston's summer home near Scotland Neck]. The team is to be driven out—and all the wheels on the plantation—lest they should be able to haul supplies to their boats. He charged them in his absence to remember their duty to me and to give me no trouble. They were much affected—and poor things in much fright—for they know that they are the objects sought after by these miscalled philanthropists. They entreated me not to leave them and I have promised to remain at home and take what care I can of them. I commenced packing up the most valuable things in the house preparatory to removing them to a place of safety—comparative safety, I mean, for our population is too thin to make much of a resistance should they come in force.

February 14—The mail tonight brought Mr. Edmondston a commission as Lieutenant Colonel of Cavalry, in the service of the Confederate States! Ah, me—I ought to be happier than I am but the prospect of long and uncertain separations eclipses, for the moment, the glory of serving his country. After all, I am but an "Earthen Vessel." But courage—I will be worthy of my blood—of my husband. I will be glad—I am glad, glad that he can serve that land to which we owe so much—our home—our native land!

How differently has this Valentine's Day been passed from the last! Then I was peacefully planting fruit trees at Hascosea ... today in the face of a stern reality am I packing up my household goods to remove them from the enemy!

February 15—I went up to Father's to dinner. As we stopped at the door we were surprised to see the windows of the dining room crowded with little faces, watching our descent from the carriage. On entering the drawing room two strange ladies sprang up and met us with the exclamation: "Where did you come from?"

We soon found that they were refugees—and thought that we were in the same sad situation. Poor people, they have been driven from their homes by the advance of the enemy —and are now seeking an asylum. . . . Nineteen whites and seventy negroes—all homeless. . . . Poor Mama—I was truly sorry for her. She had commenced packing her linen and valuables when this influx of people came upon her. She could not be persuaded quietly to accept it!—to go on with her preparations and give them what was most easily obtained. . . . No, she worried herself to prepare a handsome dinner and an elaborate dessert—and whilst actually threatened with invasion and loss of almost everything. I believe Pherebe's carelessness in spilling water in some apple jelly . . . and Mary Clark's mischief in pulling the furniture of her room out of place worried her more than Burnside and his host.

February 16—The roads are crowded with refugees in vehicles of every kind—endeavoring to move what of their property they can. Raining all day but the work of moving goes steadily on—terrible work it is too—with the roads in the state they are, and only oxen to do everything.

March 3—A note from Mr. Shaw telling me that Austin's house burned, and that he lost everything he had—poor fellow. Blankets, clothes—beds—in fact, everything. Where are more to come from I am sure I cannot tell, but that does not distress Cuffee—Master must build him a house and give him wherewithal to make himself comfortable. Ah! Mrs. Stowe, when you drew your picture you should have put in some of the lights of Cuffee's life—not all shadow.

March 17—Found the hyacinths in most beautiful bloom! They are truly exquisite, and as we came into the gate and their fragrance stole over us the charm of a quiet home never seemed greater. As they looked up to us in their peaceful beauty, smiling in the midst of these war's alarms, it made us prize our seclusion the more!

March 18—Rode over to Hascosea with Patrick. Our road lay through the woods and over old fields. How melancholy they seem—the hands that cultivated them and the heads that planned the cultivation now all mouldering in the grave —yet still the furrow remains. How true are the words of the Psalmist, "They call the lands after their own names"— for so many of these fields are known by names—long extinct among the living—the memory of man runneth not back to the time of their proprietorship. Alas, how sad to think that these fields which we now cultivate with so much pleasure—this property we now view with so much pride— may some day be like these fields—a place for the bittern and the stork to congregate.

March 26—A furor of marriage seems to possess the plantation. On Thursday, Fanny, after bustling aimlessly about the room, came out with "Master Joe—Joe Axe from the ferry wants to see you—he wants to axe you and Miss to let him marry me." So Joe was admitted into the dining room, the preliminaries settled, and they left with the permission to fix their own time. This was of the shortest, for the next day I was called on for the materials for the wedding supper. Then on Sunday came Dempsey with a request for Rachel . . . on Wednesday Lorenzo Dow to marry Mela . . . and on Thursday Hercules with a similar request for Chloe. So Cupid gave place to Hymen in a shorter time than usual. Primitive customs, one will say. But Cuffee strips off the elegancies and refinements of civilization with great ease. White people would have been months in accomplishing what they have been days about!

April 2—Andy Johnson made military Governor of Tennessee, an insult to the people. Little did my old grandfather—

when he sent his coachman to whip him and his cousins, altogether known as Jesse Johnson's boys, back to their cabin because they had a fancy to run naked on the road—ever think he would reach such a height!

April 5—Went to Hascosea and found them planting corn. The long mooted question is settled—we plant only forty acres—last year 300. Ah—Mother England, you little know the misery in store. You think you can raise the blockade when you will, and relieve your suffering children, but Mistress of the Sea as you are—what will you do when there is no cotton and no corn? All because you resolutely closed your eyes to injustice, and to oppression which you profess to abhor!

Our people suffer terribly from extortioners and speculators—"Army Worms" they are called. Salt 28 dollars, sugar 25 cents, butter 75 cents, beef 30. Shoes and leather almost fabulous. But we must curb our wants. Our Grandmothers for seven years had no pins—actually dressed with thorns! I remember my grandmother used to tell us that in the village in which she lived there was but one needle—this sewed everything, and went the rounds of the village.

April 15—Beauregard's call for plantation bells to be cast into cannon is most cheerfully responded to by every one. Church bells are freely and gladly tendered by the congregations. Preserving kettles are joyfully given to make into caps. One little child asked plaintively as she saw the preserving kettle going, "But what shall we do for preserves?" "My child," said the father, "we think now only of preserving our country!" I wonder what her idea of a preserved country is? I warrant she thinks it a large peach.

May 10—Wherever the Yankees are they encourage the Negroes to join them and tell them they are free. But they are beginning to be disgusted with them themselves. The

Negro thinks he is as good as a Yankee—and is insolent in proportion.

About Fortress Monroe they have proclaimed Emancipation and allowed the Negro to appropriate the house and property of their masters. Mrs. Dave's servant walks about New Bern with a lease of his mistress' house in his pocket. He has actually *leased* it to a Yankee official.

May 18—Came home with Patrick in a canoe. Just as we left came the mail—New Orleans has indeed fallen—fallen—and to two gun-boats. Came home deeply dejected—nay, humiliated! Patrick much discouraged about the battalion. He fears it will not succeed.

This Conscript Act is a hard one. It commences too young; the President himself says it is "like grinding seed corn" to allow boys to enter the Army—and yet he calls for all over eighteen—twenty to forty would, I think, be better. But, then, Mrs. Edmondston, you are not of the cabinet.

And the terrible fall of New Orleans coming so unexpectedly! What a blow it is. Sugar gone—Texas beef gone—leather—horses—all lost to us! Now indeed begins the War of Endurance. Let me write the names of my commanders! Endurance—Patience—Cheerfulness—Faith—these be the captains under whose banner I enlist.

May 20—Talleyrand's saying that in public matters a blunder is worse than a crime seems to be true about the surrender of Norfolk. Few crimes could have spread the distress that that has on this whole section. Most of the money in circulation was Norfolk money—all our crops are sold there, and it is the general exchange. Many have all of their ready money in the hands of Norfolk merchants—not only unavailable, but in danger of total loss,—God help the poor. We can wear old clothes and live off the plantation for years if we can only get salt—but what is to become of those who have no such resources?

May 22—I have just read Butler's infamous proclamation about the ladies of New Orleans and cannot find words to express my horror and indignation: "For the information of this army, the following General Order, No. 28, of the Federal officer, Major General Butler, commanding at New Orleans, will be read on dress parade: As the officers and soldiers of the United States have been subject to repeated insults, from the women, calling themselves ladies of New Orleans, in return for the most scrupulous non-interference and courtesy on our part, it is ordered that, hereafter, when any female shall by word, gesture, or movement insult or show contempt for any officer or soldier of the United States, she shall be regarded and held liable to be treated as a woman of the town, plying her vocation. By command of Major General Butler, May 19, 1862." Good God! Have we come to this? Even though our foes should be those of our own households, we have a spirit unconquerable—invincible! We have severed all bonds . . . we desire naught from you— we detest you!

June 6—General Lee has issued an order to the army in which he tells them that "there will be no more retreating." The watchword is Victory or Death!

June 12—The Yankees have in and about New Bern more than 6,000 Negroes who work when they please—and if they do not please they draw their rations from Quartermaster. This cannot last—no government can stand it—the end must soon come. Burnside is arming and drilling the Negroes and expects, when the fate of Richmond is decided, to commence active operations. God be with us!

June 29—Sunday—Went to church but there was no service, Mr. Cheshire having been sent for to bury a young man, one of his Tarboro congregation whose body was brought from the battlefield yesterday. Another house plunged into grief and mourning by this needless cruel war!

July 1–The battle [of Richmond] still rages. McClellan certainly in retreat to the James—Jackson on one flank—Longstreet on the other—and Magruder and Hill pressing him in front. God be with our poor wounded! The sight is pitiable in the extreme. Every house is shàttered with shot or shell. Yet amidst the ruins are huddled our own and the enemy's wounded for they no longer attempt to carry them with them but are forced by our advance to abandon them. Dispatched all the hospital stores I have—linen, cotton, wine, cordial, etc., to Richmond, praying that they might alleviate some poor fellow's sufferings. Our anxiety intense!

July 3–Out of 15,000 wounded Yankees in one hospital one third are wounded in the back! There is valour for you. They fight well, however, as our dead testify.

July 13–Yesterday came home Patrick. He gives a most moving account of the suffering in Richmond! He says it is fearful! The hot weather . . . the crowded hospitals . . . the stench . . . the want of attendance . . . the filthy muddy James River water—tepid at that! The actual want of proper food—altogether make an amount of human suffering difficult to conceive of. And then add to that the desolation of heart—the anguish endured by those who have lost friends or have them suffering, unable to alleviate their pain, and it makes a picture of war from which one turns appalled! Twice since he has been gone did he see ladies going on to nurse their husbands—one of whom heard of the death of hers in the [railroad] cars and the other saw a coffin marked with the name of hers carried past her as she sat by the window!

July 14–Have just been overlooking the work on the flax—having the seed stripped off. We have a good crop and the fibres seem strong. I will get a wheel and learn to spin it—at least make towels and gloves.

July 21–Anniversary of the Battle of Manassas. No one would have thought one year ago that this war would still be raging and the blockade still unraised. Thanks to Patrick's far seeing, I suffer less than my neighbors. Shoes for the servants I need most—but the weather is warm and they can go barefoot—though I do not like it. Today my handmaidens made their advent into the house thus, to their infinite delight. The price of shoes is such as to prohibit us from the maids trampling under foot from ten to fifteen dollars.

July 22—Sent to Wilmington for cards and sugar. Think of it! Got a pair of cards and four pounds of sugar for twelve dollars.

July 28—Came the news of the passage of the Conscript Act—which puts all men under forty-five under the command of the president. Mr. E. is under forty-five, but I will not weaken myself by looking forward to his being placed in the ranks. The same mail brought the announcement that Mr. Lincoln has declared the slaves of all *Rebels* free! to take effect on the first of January, 1863. God be with us and keep us from internal, as well as external foes.

October 11—Saw Mr. Cannon—from Perquimans. He gives a deplorable account of the state of affairs in the eastern counties. At least ten thousand Negroes have been stolen or enticed off from their owners since the fall of Roanoke Island. All our acquaintances have lost their men—many of them their Negro women also. A gentleman friend of Mr. Cannon—one whom he considers reliable—told him that in a ride from Sunbury to Suffolk—a distance of twenty-eight miles—he counted on the side of the road the corpses of fourteen Negro children left unburied for the fowls of the air to prey on. They had died from want—or sickness it may be—and deserted by their mammies and just left as they fell.

Mr. E. will be exempted from the conscript as he owns more than eighty slaves—and will only go if he gets an appointment. He has not the health nor the strength for a common soldier. . . . He has done his duty, and if he is left at home with me I am content. If the Exemption Act does not pass Father will be the only white male for fifteen miles this side of the river, and that with a population of four thousand Negroes. But we fear them little enough.

The Exemption Bill has passed! Everyone who works twenty Negroes is exempt from the Conscription Act. One white man as "Owner" or "Overseer"—on every plantation.

November 9—About three in the morning we heard the tread of a horse—and this time it proved to be John Currie with a note from Mr. Speed telling us that "time is serious . . . the Yankees advancing . . . cavalry in pursuit of our men [toward Tarboro]." We were soon dressed and down stairs. Found Mr. Currie in a state of excitement and alarm scarcely to be described! He told us that our neighbors were all moving—that a heavy land force occupied the roads whilst five gun boats were in the river—and much more to the same effect. My heart sickened within me! I felt weak and faint but thank God He gave me strength to subdue all manifestations of fear and in a short time I rallied and was enabled to go calmly to my preparations for leaving home.

About two the next afternoon we left Hascosea perhaps forever! On Thursday [the following day] Mr. Edmondston went to Clarksville to attempt to organize a company for local defense—but failed, there being but few there willing to join him. Captain Clements read him a letter from his sister, Mrs. Kinchin Taylor, telling him of the outrages they committed at her house. She said the Yankees swashed in like devils, yelling, whooping, and screaming. Her Negro servant, Ness, drew a knife and took his station by her telling them that he would kill the first man who laid a finger upon her! Noble conduct—as all who know how timid the race is generally will admit! The soldiers sacked the house—threw everything out of it breaking everything that could break and chopping the furniture to pieces. They built a fire out of doors, cut up the corn crop and threw it on it. Killed all the fattening hogs, sheep, cattle, and cows and threw them also into it. They took her carriage and every horse on the premises, telling her that they would have burned the house but that she was in it.

November 11—Salt—that is our greatest want—the greatest suffering aside from the loss of friends which this cruel war inflicts. If it be not relieved famine will cast its gaunt shadow over our land before another summer.

December 11—There is not a white soul within five miles of me, yet I have no sensation of fear.

Well, I will go to bed for it is late and I have been hard at work all day. Let me see—I got Mr. E. off early—attended to the moulding two dozen candles—lapped thread with my own hands for three yards cloth—hanked seven broaches of cotton—knit two fingers and thumb on a pair of fine white gloves for General Clark. After dinner commenced a soldier's sock—read the paper—drank tea—took a nap—finished the sock—wrote my journal—and now with a sense of something accomplished think I have earned a night's repose.

January 10, 1863—There is the story of a Negro girl, in the exercise of her Yankee-given right, who went in search of a mistress in Illinois. Said the Yankee woman to her would-be maid, "Can you cook?" "Naw, Mam—Aunt Phyllis *she* always did the cookin.'" "Can you wash?" "Naw, Mam, Aunt Judy, *she* always washed." "Can you sew?" "Naw, Mam, Aunt Myra, *she* always sewed." "Can you set the table?" "Naw, Mam, Sam, *he* always set the table." "Well, what did *you* do?" "Oh, I brushed the flies off ol' Miss."

March 5—Have been riding with Mr. E. on horseback

every afternoon for a week past, and find much benefit from it. Yesterday we saw the first plum blossom fully expanded.

The abolition Congress has passed a conscription act similar to ours, but better. Anyone can be exempt by paying three hundred dollars to the Secretary of War. Lincoln is invested with dictatorial powers in all save the name. . . . The Yankees claim to have passed Vicksburg through their boasted canal, but as it is not confirmed by our accounts, we take the liberty of disbelieving it. Their Congress has passed a bill making the treasury notes a legal tender. So Lincoln is now absolute, as he has the power of the press and the sword, besides the power to suspend the Act of Habeas Corpus.

March 28—Prices are fearfully high, even for depreciated currency—which fact, however loth and slow I am to admit it, is indisputable. Lard $1.25, bacon $6.60, and upward, flour $30.00 a barrel, tea $7.00 a pound, sugar $1.25 a pound, boots $50.00 a pair, long cloth $2.25 a yard, cotton cards $430.00 for two pair. Salt considered cheap at $25.00 a bushel, butter at $2.00 a pound, and everything else in proportion.

April—The War exercises our ingenuity. I have just finished an excellent and useful pair of gloves for Mr. E. knit of rabbit fur and wool—equal proportions spun together. They are warmer than wool and not too coarse for horseback.

May 11—The mail came in after tea and heavy news it brought us. A chill went through my heart as Mr. Edmondston unfolded the paper and I saw that it was in mourning. I felt that Stonewall Jackson was dead—and so it proved! He died of pneumonia on Sunday the 10th—eight days after the amputation of his arm. Died in the fullness of his reputation, the brightness of his glory! A Christian patriot—unselfish, untiring, with no thought but for his country, no aim but for her advancement. His very enemies reverenced him.

May 26—They [Yankees] went to Mr. Tom Newby's—my brother-in-law's uncle—an old man and feeble—and shot down his son in cold blood at his father's hearth, as he was rising from his chair with the inquiry, "Who's there?" on hearing their footsteps! He fell dead on the hearth—and they would not suffer his father to remove the body from the fire whilst they remained! They dragged the old man about with them from place to place demanding where this article and where that was which they wanted and took everything they fancied. Actually stationed themselves in his wife's bedchamber, she being sick in bed and an old lady, and mimicked her distress and her calls to her servant to come and get her her gown. When they went off they drove every Negro he owned, some of them at the point of the bayonet, and all his horses and mules before them. The only reason for their peculiar barbarity that could be found was that he had had a son—not the one they killed—formerly in the service.

July—News! News! News! So much of it that I do not know where to begin! There has been a battle—a terrible battle at Gettysburg, Pennsylvania. We get Yankee accounts of it alone, but are sure that Meade is falling back to Baltimore and Lee is pursuing him. We lost three Brigadiers—on their side the loss is heavier. Gettysburg absorbs all thought.

July 3—Mrs. Tunis of Norfolk (niece of our friend, Dr. Charles E. Johnson of Raleigh) lost all her servants by the blandishments of their Yankee confreres. One of her women left her two children—one an infant in arms, the other just able to walk, behind her. Mrs. Tunis having the whole care of her own children did not choose to be burdened with two pickaninnies, so taking one in her arms and the other by the hand she went to headquarters and desired to see General Viele. The sight of a Southern lady carrying a Negro baby gained her immediate admittance. "As these children, General Viele, have been deprived of their mother by your act, I come here to surrender them to you!" at the same time making a motion to give him the infant. "Good God! Madam!" said he, springing to his feet. "You do not mean to leave these children here with me?" "That, sir, is my intention!" And suiting the action to the word, she deposited the baby upon his table in the midst of his papers and calmly saying, "Good morning, sir," walked out and left them both behind her!

I have no heart to write! Vicksburg *has* fallen! It is all true! We are told they were reduced to the verge of starvation. The officers were allowed to march out with their side arms—retain their horses. Who ever heard of a beleaguered city starving while they had horses?

July 14—I look at our books—friends we have been years collecting—with a sigh to think that in a few days we may see them mutilated and cast out—perhaps burned—and ourselves wanderers without a home.

August 1—No news from General Lee except that he is falling back. Our loss at Gettysburg in both men and officers is terrible. The best blood in our state cries from the ground.

August 12—Two lads, one just under and the other just over sixteen, soldiers in Faison's regiment, came begging something to eat. It almost made me weep to see them. They have been sixteen months in service. Truly, as President Davis said, "It is grinding our seed corn." It was touching to see them eat! When I filled their haversacks with supper for to-night, child-like I think their gratitude was more excited by the peaches and apples than by the ham and bread with which I crammed them.

August 23—Father had a letter today from his sister, Mrs. Polk. The account she gives of the sufferings witnessed by an acquaintance of hers [a Mrs. Butler who went through the Yankee lines under a pass from Grant] of the Negroes about Vicksburg are heart-rending. She says for miles and miles the road was lined with them. The locks of the fences had been converted by means of boughs into rude shelters under which they lay on the ground dead and dying by scores. As she passed she was met by entreaties from the poor creatures that she would tell their masters to come and take them.

September 6—I was out yesterday visiting, and sad to say Death had been before me in eight households. One of the ladies whose husband had been killed at Middleburg has since lost four children of diphtheria. Out of all this sorrow, there was only one who did not trace her sorrow to this unnatural War.

September 9—Sad news of desertions from our army! Ten men were shot in front of Lee's army last week. And what humilitation indeed; they were all from a North Carolina regiment. Two regiments have been sent from Lee's army to arrest deserters in the western part of this state. Raleigh rumor has it that they are an organized body—have elected officers and entrenched themselves in a camp in Wilkes County.

September 29—Yesterday passed some hunters—"on a stand" for deer. What a thrill of old associations the sight of them awakened! Remembrances of dreamy October days . . . of woods one flush of gorgeous coloring . . . of repose deep, untroubled, and serene . . . of quiet broken only by the steady chirp of the autumn cricket chirping as he only does after the first frost . . . of dropping nuts and falling acorns . . . of plenty and prosperity . . . corn fields with tender heads awaiting the gatherer's hand . . . of, to sum it all in one word, Peace!

October 1—Father saw two of our soldiers just exchanged from David Island. They told him they had been well treated, and that they had but a single instance of shabbiness to complain of. A donation was made by some kindhearted persons of good clothing to the Confederate prisoners. The Colonel in command of the post, before issuing it, had all the skirts of the coats and the bottoms of the trousers cut off. He should be known as "Colonel Curtail."

Sue told me a laughable instance of the detestation of the Yankees in even little children. Little Laura, a saucy little four-year-old, being out of temper generally, and desiring to make an exhibition of it, began thus: "I loves rats, I does! I loves spiders, too, I does." No notice being taken she rose higher in the scale: "I loves lizards, I does! I loves snakes, too, I does. I loves Yankees, I does. Sister Nan, did you hear me? I loves Yankees." This was as far as she could go!

November 19—My nephew, Thomas Devereux, my brother's eldest son joined the Army last week just in time to flash his maiden sword. He was eighteen only. Where are our sons of education and science—our enlightened statesmen—our wise rulers to come from—when our youths of eighteen are snatched from their studies? Their minds are but half disciplined, their intellectual development but half completed, their memories but half stored. Though my young countrymen may not be so skilled in the learning of Greece and Rome, and the quadrature of the circle and the mysteries of the conic section may be a sealed book to them, let us trust that they will bring back from the battlefield a knowledge of men, of the secret springs of the human heart; and fitted, as they will be by having learned obedience, to govern, the future of our country in their hands will be both glorious and prosperous. That *War*, while she strips from them many a modern refinement, and the wisdom of schools, will gild them with her own barbaric virtues—a lofty contempt of danger, a chivalric devotion to women, a spirit of self-sacrifice which will make them spring to the defense of the weak, a devotion to their country, a love of honor which shall be their guiding star through life.

February 19, 1864—Our Wedding Day! Our one great anniversary of the year. Came home last night, though bitterly cold, to keep it alone at home. Hands busy all day filling the ice house—and if we can judge from present prospects it will keep well. But half a Wedding Day. This tiresome business of the runaway Negroes having absorbed half. James Bartley (nearly sixty years of age) seems to be the prime mover. He, by the inducement of a fine suit of clothes and a pair of boots, has persuaded several of Father's prime hands to desert and run off to the Yankees. Lewis and Hilliard seem to have been the pioneers but Dow, Edgar, Rimson, and Joe Spier are so deeply incriminated that today they go off to Richmond [to be sold]. Joe Axe, the husband of my maid Fanny, and many others are by no means free from suspicion —but it has been decided on account of their youth to deal more mildly with them. Hood Manuel, an ivory-headed old traitor, it has been decided to keep, and by his aid to arrest the arch apostate "Cumbo." The Yankees give him two hundred dollars for every able-bodied Negro he brings in to them.

April 18—Recently in Mississippi we attacked a Regiment of mounted Cuffies and not one was left to tell the tale. The Negroes have a hard time in the Yankee service—put by their new masters in the front, they bear the brunt of the day, and do not receive from their old masters the quarter or the mercy shown by them to prisoners of war but are shot down without hesitation, not allowed even to surrender. We desire to have no complications on the subject of Negro exchanges!

May 19—One anecdote of the Army of Northern Virginia which has reached us I must record. During one of the recent battles General Lee placed himself at the head of a Texas Brigade in order to lead them into battle when, as one man they halted and cried out, "We will not advance unless you go back!" Was ever a nobler tribute paid by men to a Commander?

May 25—I walk in my garden where one hundred and twelve varieties of rose, all in splendid bloom salute me, and think how many of our noble young countrymen have closed their eyes forever to all scenes of earthly beauty! How the sight of such blaze of splendour would fall cold on the hearts of thousands of my country-women who weep—whilst I linger along these fragrant walks enjoying the delicious perfume and letting my eye rest admiringly on the beauty around me.

May 30—If I dwell on the behavior of my Yankee brethren I shall be in a fair way to emulate Mama's condition. She said with great earnestness a few days since, "I declare! If this war continues much longer I shall lose the little Christianity I have got!"

June 5—I have just read a letter . . . from Captain Skinner to his sister, my niece, Mrs. Jones. It is dated "Front line of Entrenchments near Old Church, May 31st." He says in it, "Pattie, we have had a dreadful time and all is not yet over but I hope the worst is passed. Grant has been taught such a severe lesson by Lee and his ragged rebels that he is the most cautious man to be found. Battle has been offered him a half a dozen times since leaving Spotsylvania Court House but he has not accepted. This army is in fine condition and overflowing spirits—notwithstanding that we have lost heavily and suffered untold hardships. Until the 29th we lived on 4 crackers and a ¼ pound of meat per day—but now our rations have been doubled and all are jubilant though before that happy event there was but a murmur to be heard—and yet men in my company were whole days at a time without a morsel. We are all dirty and if you will pardon the expression—lousy—having been twenty-five days without a change of clothing. During this time we have marched —counter marched—fought, etc., without intermission.... Don't be distressed. I am perfectly contented, and if I can hear from you and our mother occasionally I am really happy. Don't imagine that because a battle is impending that we are long-faced and miserable. On the contrary we are cheerful ... I firmly believe that I will pass through unharmed.... If you love me, don't be troubled but trust all to God and pray for your dear brother Ben."

How can such men ever be conquered!

[Later in June]—Oh, that we had Peace! This constant anxiety and watching must tell on our men. How does General Lee suffer it? God's blessing only—and God's strength enables him to bear up. What a position does he occupy— the idol—the point of trust—of confidence and repose of thousands! How nobly has he won the confidence, the admiration of the Nation. I remember when General Joe Johnston was wounded at Seven Pines, and Lee in consequence took the head of the army himself—many persons—both doubted his ability in the field—and deplored his removal from the cabinet. An excellent one to plan and lay out a campaign—but with too little energy to carry it out! They even called him "Old-stick-in-the-mud." Should anyone now dare to remember or to apply that sobriquet to him, their heads to a certainty would be broken—if not by one of his men, by a civilian; such is the confidence and affectionate trust we all repose in him. "Marse Robert" can do anything and all things!

August—I have referred to the "Solitaire" but I have never described it. We have had a small house in the garden, known to the rest of the world as a tool house, fitted up privately as a withdrawing room—a couch, a table, two

chairs, an ink stand—a portfolio—a vase of flowers—a shelf—
a few books and a broom constitute its whole furniture. Here
Mr. E. and I retire when we wish to be absolutely alone . . .
and here I have taken my Bible, prayer book, and journal,
and with the perfume of sweet flowers around me, I can
daily read and lift up my heart in gratitude, better than I
can in the house. . . . I come in and find some little evidence
that he has been before me—a peach or a pear—or a book left
open at the page he has been reading. I go out and leave
a memento for him—a rose—a vase of flowers—a half-writ-
ten letter—and the air of secrecy and seclusion gives it a
double zest. It is like "stolen fruit" or "bread eaten in secret."

October 30—Got Mr. E. ready to take the field—provisions
for several days—packed his carpet satchel, overhauled his
military accoutrements, and resolutely kept down all the sad
forebodings which in spite of me would rise in my heart and
almost choke me. He came in at dinner and electrified me
with the tidings that Lieutenant Morley, commandant of the
"Albemarle," had blown her up! . . . The fashion set by Commander Fatnall must be followed by every other numbskull
in the Confederate Navy who, like him, gets drunk and
neglects his duty. . . . From all we know now, it was a
disgraceful business. Plymouth was conquered by Apple
Brandy (drunk by whom, I hope a court martial will find
out). This is the verdict of the neighborhood.

November 3—The capture of Plymouth hangs like a pall
on our spirits. God's will be done, and grant us faith to see
His hand in it, and to know that state in which He places
us is the one in which it is best for us to be!

November 15—Have planted two squares in my garden
with tea, so we shall in a few years be independent of the
blockade. I have also done what I should have done years
ago—made a large fig plantation. Some of these days I will
rival Smyrna in my own dried figs—who knows? All quiet

along our lines. There is little doubt that Mr. Lincoln is reelected President of the United States.

November 17—I yesterday went to see Father, and for the first time in my life drove myself in the buggy. I was not well enough to ride horseback.

President Davis in his late message suggests the propriety of taking forty thousand slaves and making pioneer laborers and engineers of them—hinting at the promise of ultimate freedom—and pointing plainly to the fact that should we find it necessary to arm our slaves—this forty thousand trained and disciplined body would be the nucleus of the organization. Can one credit it? . . . But that silly Congress should consume their time and our money in a grave discussion over the best means to destroy the country is a depth of folly too deep for me to fathom!

. . . Thus it is to be for some years to come—every man of small caliber has come home a hero with a string of adventures as long as a three volume novel, which he insists on pouring into your ear. It is a terrible bore.

December 25—A proclamation from Governor Vance calling on every man "who can handle a musket, or stand behind a breastwork" to rally at Wilmington for its defense, so this morning Mr. E. packed a few things in his satchel and taking his blanket and the Governor's orders is off to report to General Leaventhorpe for duty.

December 27—Last night came the tidings of the fall of Savannah. "Successfully evacuated"—nothing more. So fall all our hopes. We know nothing of the force we had, nothing of our casualties. We form no judgment or opinion of the event. . . . Mr. E. is off again tomorrow. He would go today but his buggy is broken and his horse tired out. I must prepare rations for a long absence from home for him. He gave me minute directions about his business and the management of the plantation in his absence, so I hope that I will be able to carry it on as it should be done.

December 30—One of the saddest results of our situation is a letter from General Lee to Mr. Miles, chairman of the military commission in Congress, advising the conscription-emancipation and arming of 200,000 slaves immediately. It proves to me that General Lee knows more of setting an army in the field than he does of Cuffee. Our country is ruined if he adopts his suggestion. We give up a principle when we offer emancipation as a reward or boon, for we have hitherto contended that slavery was Cuffee's normal condition, the very best position he could occupy, the one of all others in which he was the happiest, and to take from him that and give him what we think is misery, is to put ourselves in the wrong. This Negro question—this vexed Negro question—will, if longer discussed, do us more harm than the loss of a battle.

I am reading Lord Bacon's essays regularly through—one every day. What a mine of thought they are!

January 22, 1865—Ah! that Ft. Fisher had stood! The elements on our side we might have struck a signal blow. The discontent with the [Confederate] Government increases. Revolution—the deposition of Davis is openly talked of! Who can tell how it will all end—vain are our conjectures. We wait with folded hands what is in store for us. God grant that it be neither emancipation or subjugation.

January 29—As for Blair's return, so little hope have I of any results from negotiations whilst they are now triumphant that I believe I failed to mention the fact that he was in Richmond with a proposition for peace. Peace with them just now means subjugation and abolition of slavery—neither of which we are ready to submit to.

February 9—Our commissioners have indeed returned,

having been met at Fortress Monroe by Mr. Lincoln and his wily secretary, Mr. Seward. The interview took place on board a steamboat—our commissioners not being allowed to land. Mr. Lincoln utterly refuses to treat with our authorities as it would be a recognition of them. The terms he informally offers us are submission, entirely, utterly and abjectly to the United States. Then an adoption of the new and remarkable constitution of their country, just passed by the Federal Congress, one clause of which is the abolition of slavery in consideration of which he promises, so far as depends upon himself, a liberal and lenient construction of the pains and penalties incurred by the leaders of the Rebellion. That is, I believe, all. Mr. Lincoln related a few anecdotes—was reminded of a "man in Illinois" once or twice, shook hands with our commission. Seward, the hypocrite, wished them God's blessing, drank a bottle of champagne with them, when up steam, and Ho! for Richmond!

February 14—One thing deeply pains me, i.e., the growing distrust with which all men view the Government. It is getting to be considered an instrument of oppression and tyranny because it does not keep faith with its citizens. The Conscript Act was a breach of promise, the act diminishing the value of money was another, and now this last fatal step of refusing to accept its own bonds in discharge of its demands will, I fear, breed more mischief. It takes owners' whole surplus at its own price, and for sole equivalent gives you a piece of yellow paper, refuses to give you a circulating medium, and immediately after that comes another agent, demands I know not what per cent of tax on your property and absolutely refuses to look at your demand on the Government. In private life that would be called *swindling*.

Mr. E. at Clarksville yesterday. When he came in he had a sad state of things to relate to me. Our neighbor's Negroes have either taken a panic or become demoralized and are going off by tens and twenties to the Yankees. All farm hands. The intimation which they have had from the free discussion of putting them in the army—which many of them had heard from their masters whilst waiting on table—has so frightened and excited them that some of them went off without preparation, making a Hegira more sudden than that of the Israelites from Egypt. We see no effect of the panic on our people. Probably the extreme isolation in which we keep them has prevented their being affected by it.

February 19—More bad news of the state of feeling among the Negroes. All of our neighbors have suffered. Nearly a hundred crossed the river last night. Our time seems not to have come yet, but who can tell how many hours it will be delayed. The wolf is at our throat. These Negroes will carry an account of our defenseless condition and of our plentiful land and abundant crops. Mr. E. at Halifax all day in compliance with the order to reorganize the Home Guard. One of the newly elected lieutenants was so drunk that he knew not how to comport himself, and the new captain is by no means sober.

February 25—I hard at work alone all day turning one of his thick overcoats! Think of it! Did I ever in former days think that I would come to sewing or he to wearing a turned coat. However it looks nice and I am thankful that it is worth the labour.

Breckinridge has been made Secretary of War. I am sorry we lose him from the field. Napoleon believed in *luck,* and Breckenridge is not only able, but lucky.

March 2—The House has passed the Negro Enlistment Bill—making it however voluntary with the masters whether they send their slaves or not. Deprecates any action which interferes with the rights of the owners. Authorizes the President to *ask* for the slaves only. An attempt of our wise Congress to "Run with the hare, and hunt with the hounds."

An attempt which will end in utter failure to do either. Our legislation during the war has truly been a series of millstones hung needlessly around our necks.

March 11—Mr. Davis is out in a stirring proclamation assuring us that we are not and will not be subjugated—exhorting us to stand firm. Yesterday came the impressing officers with orders to *take all the best* of our teams, to leave us only the worthless and the inferior. This morning the two best mules we have here were taken, and as I write, I see six of the team at Looking Glass and Mr. E.'s new blooded filly for which he gave $5000 but two months since coming, a sad procession, to join those already impressed! . . . What is to become of our eighty-five Negroes thus deprived of food and employment? The Government says, "Make them work with hoes." But suppose we have no hoes, and no means of getting them? What then?

March 15—On consultation last week we had determined to deprive ourselves of meat at one meal per diem and to give what we save to the army; but the need is so pressing that we go beyond that and give 500 pounds of meat and 1500 pounds of meal which we had intended for our own table, and we live on bread and vegetables. I must bestir myself and make every inch of my garden do its full duty.

In Raleigh all public buildings and even churches have been seized for hospitals. Mrs. Miller writes that she has cooking done for 280 patients in the Episcopal Church.

April 5—Whilst at dinner today enter Fanny saying, "Daddy say to come here and tell you that the Yankees are comin' and that they are burnin' Mr. Jacob's house now!" Mr. Jacob's house is just four miles from us on the other side of the river and the gunboat is their probable objective point—only a mile from us on this side! So we sit in the momentary expectation of hearing the report of cannon and the hissing of a shell to announce that the attack on the boat has commenced.

What may be our fate ere another morning! I hope when the time of trouble comes that I shall not "greatly fear."

April 6—Came news late last night—news that I cannot realize—it falls on my outward ear but I do not believe that it fully enters into my inner sense. Lee after four days' heavy fighting in which the slaughter on both sides has been terrific has evacuated Petersburg.... God help us—we are in the crisis of our fate as a nation!

April 16—How can I write it! How find words to tell what has befallen us! *General Lee has surrendered*.... Surrendered the remnant of his noble army to an overwhelming horde of mercenary Yankee knaves and foreigners!

That Lee, Lee upon whom hung the hopes of the whole country, should be a prisoner seems too dreadful to be realized. Grant, it is said, issued a special order enjoining his troops to spare his life and to offer him no indignity—and at the surrender refused to accept his sword, saying he was not worthy to receive it, and released him on his simple parole. But he is lost to us. Noble old man, we almost forget our own loss in sympathy with you! He has not been out-maneuvered nor out-generaled, but crushed, crushed by mere brute force —force he could no more resist than he could the fall of an avalanche. We but love him the more for his misfortunes.

Since we heard of the disaster I seem as though in a dream —a kind of a "drowsy dream." I sleep—sleep—sleep—endlessly. If I sit in my chair ten minutes, I doze. I sit benumbed. It is to me like a simple mental assent without once comprehending it, or even feeling it. I sit and hear Mrs. Langdon and the young folks talk of books and poetry, and they seem to be talking of what was long, long ago. I read books—I liked poetry—when was it? Where are they all gone? In the vain attempt to grasp it I fall asleep. I am not dejected—not cast down. Seemingly the loss of New Orleans and of Vicksburg affected me much more. What is it that sustains me? Not faith in the Army. That is gone—that band of heroes has melted away. Is it faith in Mr. Davis? I have not felt that since he removed General Johnston. *I believe it is faith in the country.*

April 23—The rule which the Yankees keep over Cuffee astonished him greatly—the whip with which the Yankee vice-provost has armed himself is one which no Southern overseer ever dared use—even own. The only instrument ever used on our Negroes was a switch cut from some neighboring bush—and these new punishments, bull whips, hanging by the thumbs, and bucking astonish them greatly.

June 26—The Yankees tell them that freedom does not mean "freedom from work," but freedom from the lash and from the degradation of being sold. Now, as but few of them have ever felt the first to any appreciable degree, and as the second always secured them a comfortable home and an assured subsistence, they prefer a degradation which they cannot understand to being turned adrift and told to shift for themselves. They have taxed their masters' patience beyond human endurance. They occupy themselves ceaselessly trying on their new chains—seeing how little work they can accomplish and yet be fed, and endeavoring to be slave and free at the same moment—a slave on the food, shelter and clothing question, but free when labour is concerned.

October 1—During the whole of my sickness I was nursed in a most devoted and affectionate manner by my maid, Fanny. At times she actually wept over me, and with the most earnest and tender solicitude she constantly cared for me. And yet—when I was scarce able to walk without assistance—she left me without provocation or reason—left me in the night, and that too without the slightest notice.

. . . The better sort amongst them are beginning to see that they have been duped and, disappointed in their expectation of land and teams and implements, are becoming soured and discontented to a degree not at all surprising. A feeling of animosity and antagonism against their masters is sedulously cultivated by the Bureau. Our foreman—Henry—one of the most intelligent of his class is much changed, and in place of his affectionate and cheerful simplicity of manner and speech he has become moody and discontented—thinks he ought to have land because his forefathers cleared and he worked it. Can't believe his "Governor" is going to give him his bare freedom with nothing to maintain it.

December 31—So ends this terrible year of 1865. Thank God it is over! So now to our egg-nog and brighter hopes for 1866.

CHAPTER SEVEN

Some Kindness Lightened Even Prisons

IN SOME WARS WE ARE TOLD THAT BATTLE SO RAVAGED THE *soldier's mind and body that it was sometimes a relief to be captured. Terrible as was Civil War fighting, this was rarely true of Confederate or Union soldiers. For to most even the risk of battle was preferred to days and months and years slowly passing as the bodies of the prisoners shrank from starvation or disease. And yet, such was the stubborn courage of many men on both sides, they endured it and lived to tell tales of horror or kindness or even humor that never failed to fascinate their audiences.*

The Rebels who were captured during the war discovered that there were good Yankees as well as bad ones. Henry P. Rudasill of Catawba County, North Carolina, met with unexpected sympathy as well as hardship at the hands of his Northern captors as he indicates in these reminiscences of his adventures as a prisoner:

I lost my arm at Winchester, September 13th, 1864, and was captured at the same time and sent to the Federal Hospital. There I remained for a month and received good treatment. The ladies of the town would bring all kinds of delicacies suitable for the sick and wounded. One month from the time I was captured, our forces attempted to re-take Winchester, and all of us prisoners expected to be liberated. In the excitement, I walked out of the hospital to a three-story Southern mansion, where I was hidden in the third story; but when Sheridan drove Early back, I returned to the hospital, where I, with others of the wounded prisoners, were reported as deserters. All of us who were able to be moved were sent in wagons to Harper's Ferry and from there on the train to Baltimore Hospital.

We were in Baltimore for three weeks where we also received splendid treatment. But on the day we left, we were marched out into a very large room where all our clothing, money, etc., were taken from us and we were taken to a large pile of cast-off Federal uniforms and commanded to dress. The pants that I received were all bloody, and the right leg ripped to the knee. One poor fellow from Georgia, wounded in the shoulder and with gangrene so bad you could see the bones, had four five-dollar gold pieces, which he hid in the bowl of a large pipe. He filled it with tobacco and began to smoke; but when the Yanks came around to search him, the first place they looked was in the pipe, which they confiscated along with the gold.

When I left Baltimore I was strong and my arm was doing fine, but when I got to Savannah my wound was so swollen and I was so weak, I had to be carried off the boat. During the twenty-two days I was on the boat, my arm was washed but once and that time with a pint of stolen water. . . .

The physicians on the boat had the prisoners' wounds washed and dressed regularly, but all were bathed in the same water, and as quite a few of the soldiers had gangrene, Silas Smyre and I refused to have our wounds washed in the polluted water. . . .

Another prisoner had both good and bad experiences at the hands of the Federals. Jacob Andrew Hartsfield volunteered for service in the Army of Northern Virginia in 1861. In May of 1864 he was captured in the Battle of Spotsylvania Courthouse. In his war recollections he tells his story:

They sent me to the old Capitol Prison, Washington, D. C., where I remained thirty days. The prison fare was very good at this place. After thirty days we were sent to Fort Delaware and there we found the fare not good, two meals a day, bread the size of an ordinary loaf, half a loaf each meal, and I judged it to be made up of corn meal and flour; about eight ounces of beef per day; soup or beef water, in summer too thick with flies for use. Those who were unable to get outside help had a hard time.

Early in August there were rumors of sending 600 officers down to Charleston to be placed on Morris Island between the Union batteries and under the fire of Confederate guns. This was done in retaliation because our authorities had notified them that Yankee prisoners had to be quartered in the city [where they were in danger of being shot by their own men]. The officers of my company and others to the number of 600 were called out and sent on shipboard and steamed away to Charleston with a gunboat as convoy. Things went nice and smooth, the weather being fine, until off Cape Romain above Charleston about three or four A.M., the ship was suddenly turned at right angles, run in near the Cape, and grounded. They put the pilot in irons for this it is said. If he did it in order for us to escape, he should have given a hint of it as we didn't know where we were, nor the convoy, and dared not take advantage of the opportunity.

... It was a great relief when we finally left the ship. Being placed in a stockade laid off in streets with tents, we were guarded by Negro troops at this place commanded by white

officers. The Negro troops seemed to be more humane than
their officers.

. . . A good many wrote home for boxes and received them
in a few weeks, which was a godsend for notice soon came
that we were to be put on bread and water for forty days.
The order was soon put in force and the ration was ten
ounces corn meal and two of flour. The corn meal was about
two years old and had black lumps all through it. There was
great suffering among the men and but for the humanity of a
certain Yankee officer it would have been worse. When we
were moved from the fort, numbers of men were suffering
from scurvy and some unable to walk.

*Some prisoners, of course, lived lives of unrelieved misery.
Mrs. Charles I. Miller of South Carolina reports the experiences of Captain Thomas B. Martin: "After undergoing great
hardships, he and 500 other officers were held in stockades
on Morris Island, S. C. Here they lived in small army tents
and were fed cooked rations. Their evening meal consisted
of a scrap of bacon and a pint of mush made of spoiled corn-
meal. One evening Captain Martin counted 365 worms and
14 bugs in his portion of mush. He said he could have
counted more, but felt he could not afford to lose more of
one meal. He ravenously devoured the rest. The only water
the prisoners had was from holes dug in the sand of the
island, salty and unpalatable."*

*Lucky was the prisoner who escaped—and lived to get
back to his own lines. Mrs. H. C. Pittman of Georgia remembers the story of her great uncle Daniel Spence and his bold
break for freedom:*

When Uncle Daniel was captured, the prisoners knew
they would be shot or hanged. One man could play the
fiddle, so one night they decided they might as well make the

best of it and have some fun if they could. They were square dancing to the music of the fiddle when Uncle Daniel and a fellow prisoner decided to try to escape, although they knew they would be shot instantly if discovered. While everyone was making merry and the guards were off-guard, Uncle Daniel and his fellow prisoner climbed over the prison wall and to safety. They were so far away before they were missed that they were not found. Finally Uncle Daniel got home—tired, hungry and footsore. . . . In his last days he would ask Daddy to bring his fiddle and play for him, because a fiddle once saved his life.

One remarkable North Carolinian regularly risked his life to help Confederate prisoners escape. Mrs. Jessie Seagroves tells this story:

Joshua Moon, Jr., was a wagoner by trade, a trade which enabled him to render a heroic service to the South. Joshua hauled and sold supplies behind enemy lines. This camouflaged his real purpose. What he really did was to help escaped Rebel prisoners get back into their own territory. After unloading his load, Joshua and his young son Columbus would fill the wagon bed with tree boughs. According to a previous arrangement with Rebel prisoners he had been able to alert, Joshua dropped the tree boughs at road forks to indicate which way he was traveling. By day Joshua and young Columbus would ride alone. Once they were stopped by a Yankee officer who asked them what was the "meaning of the wagon bed of tree boughs." Joshua told him that the boy had done it, that it was just a "fool notion" of his. This answer must have sounded plausible because the Yankee let them go on. The prisoners walked by day (hiding in the woods) and rode with Joshua by night. "Dixie and the land of cotton" must have looked mighty good to these war weary prisoners when they crossed into it.

One of the most unusual experiences of a Confederate prisoner happened to the relative of a good friend of the writer's. Dr. Paul B. Barringer told the tale in his delightful book The Natural Bent:

General Rufus Barringer was the first captured Confederate general to arrive at City Point near Richmond where Federal Headquarters were established. Shortly afterward Lincoln made the place a visit.

One evening the commandant formally presented General Barringer to the President of the United States in the adjutant general's tent. Mr. Lincoln extending his hand, warmly welcomed the Confederate general, and bade him be seated. "Well, well," Lincoln said, "Your brother was my chum in Congress. Yes, sir, we sat at the same desk and ate at the same table. He was a Whig and so was I. He was my chum, and I was very fond of him. Well . . . Shake again. . . ."

Finally the General arose and was bowing himself out when President Lincoln took him again by the hand and, laying the other hand on his shoulder, said with great seriousness and simplicity, "Do you think I could be of any service to you?" All laughed and General Barringer replied with difficulty, "If anyone could be of service to a poor devil in my situation, I presume you are the man." Mr. Lincoln drew a card from his pocket, adjusted his glasses, and turned up the wick of the lamp. Then, seating himself at the desk, he wrote with all the seriousness with which he might have signed the Emancipation Proclamation. While writing, he kept up a running conversation to this effect, "I suppose they will send you to Washington and there, I have no doubt, they will put you in the old Capitol prison. I am told it isn't a nice sort of place and I am afraid you won't find it a very comfortable tavern; but I have a friend in Washington—he's the biggest man in the country—and I believe I have some influence with him when I don't ask too much. Now I want you to send this card of introduction to him and if he takes the notion, he may put you on parole, or let up on you that way or some other way. Anyway it's worth trying." Then very deliberately drying the card with the blotter, he held it up to the light and read:

This is General Barringer, of the Southern Army. He is the brother of a very dear friend of mine. Can you do anything to make his detention in Washington as comfortable as possible under the circumstances?

A. Lincoln

To Hon. Edwin M. Stanton,
Secretary of War.

For the common soldier in prison, survival was a daily struggle. James Huffman of the 10th Virginia Infantry was one who lived to write his reminiscences of prison life:

Elmira Camp was a very sickly place. The death rate was much higher than in the army during active hostilities. About half of us Virginians—and I think three-quarters of all the Southerners—died here in eight to ten months. A large number of North and South Carolinians had been captured at a Fort on the North Carolina coast—hale, hearty-looking fellows except that they were yellow from lying in the trenches. These men crowded us very much at first, but in two or three weeks they were nearly all gone to the hospitals, and most of them died. The well water looked pure and good but was deadly poison to our men, thousands taking chronic diarrhea from which they died. We had smallpox almost all the time. One doctor there said he killed more Rebs than any soldier at the front.

The often debated question as to the treatment of prisoners North and South has been authoritatively treated in Woodrow Wilson's History of the American People. *The following paragraph from Wilson is about conditions in the latter half of the war:*

One of the most distressing evidences of the straits the South had been brought to was the state of the prisons in which she was forced to keep the thousands of prisoners who fell into the hands of her armies. . . . Thirty thousand men died in the Confederate prisons; as many more in the prisons of the North: the numbers almost exactly in balance—in the South, 30,156 out of 196,000 who were prisoners; in the North, 30,152 out of 227,000. But the causes were different. In the Northern prisons the bitter chill of winter claimed as many lives as the rigors and privations of prison discipline. In the South there were not prisons, there were not guards, there was not food enough. Men could not be spared from the field to guard the prisons, and many thousands were crowded together under a handful of men. Proper sanitary precautions were in the circumstances impossible. The armies themselves lacked food and went without every comfort, and the prisoners could fare no better—inevitably fared worse, because they were penned within a narrow space and lacked the free air of the camp.

CHAPTER EIGHT

Diary of a Refugee in Richmond

WE NOW COME TO ONE OF THE MOST VIVID CHAPTERS IN OUR *book composed of extracts from a diary kept by Mrs. Judith McGuire while she was a refugee in Richmond, the heart of the Confederacy from 1861 to April, 1865. Mrs. McGuire was reared in Westwood, the country home of her family in Hanover County, and married the Rev. John P. McGuire, whose parishes were in Essex County. But for several years in the 1850's she and her husband had conducted the Episcopal High School of Virginia in Alexandria to which had come many of the most gifted sons of old Virginia families. The most tragic feature of her diary is found in the repeated references to the death in battle of so very many of these promising young men.*

Some of the most distinguished Southern leaders were visitors at Mrs. McGuire's Richmond home. There are glimpses of Jefferson Davis and General Lee. Particularly interesting are the references to Mrs. Robert E. Lee. One in 1861: "I never saw her more cheerful and she seems to have no doubt of our success." In 1862: "She is of course unhappy about her imprisoned son but you never hear a word from her." April, 1865: "She was in her invalid's chair but very cheerful and hopeful. 'The end is not yet,' she said. 'Richmond is not the Confederacy!'" Of Mrs. Jefferson Davis, we have this glimpse: *"Mrs. Davis sat at a table engaged in some fine needlework. She made a very favorable impression by her ease of manner, agreeable conversation, and kindness of heart."*

Mrs. McGuire secured a position as clerk in the commissary department at $125 a month at a time when turkeys sold at $50 to $100 and other provisions were similarly high. Her report of a near riot in Richmond in April, 1863, "principally of women" raiding the stores, sheds new light on a never wholly suppressed undercurrent of unhappiness which also found expression in frequent criticism of the Confederacy's leaders by some dissatisfied residents. Far more significant no doubt is Mrs. McGuire's story of a friend whose house was surrounded by 60,000 Federal troops headed by Gen. Siegel, who, with his staff, announced that he would take tea with her. "The elegant old lady retained her composure, rang the bell for her servant, and still seated, said quietly, 'John, tea for fourteen.'"

Mrs. McGuire's story is more interesting than a novel because it is told with a novelist's skill and with all the accuracy and emotion of a daily participant in one of history's supreme dramas. The extracts we print are from a book The Diary of a Southern Refugee, which had a limited circulation when published by E. J. Hale & Son in 1867, and has now been long out of print.

At Home [Alexandria, Virginia], May 4, 1861—I am too nervous, too wretched today to write in my diary, but that the employment will while away a few moments of this trying time. Our friends and neighbors have left us. Everything is broken up. . . . The homes all desolate; and yet this beautiful country is looking more peaceful, more lovely than ever, as if to rebuke the tumult of passion and the fanaticism of

man. We are left lonely indeed; our children are all gone—
the girls to Clarke, where they may be safer, and farther
from the exciting scenes which may too soon surround us;
and the boys, the dear, dear boys, to the camp, to be drilled
and prepared to meet any emergency. Can it be that our
country is to be carried on and on to the horrors of civil
war?

May 21— ... Day after tomorrow the vote of Virginia on
secession will be taken, and I, who so dearly loved this
Union, who from my cradle was taught to revere it, now
most earnestly hope that the voice of Virginia may give no
uncertain sound; that she may leave it with a shout. ...

Fairfax Court House, May 25—The day of suspense is at an
end. Alexandria and its environs, including I greatly fear,
our home, is in the hands of the enemy. Yesterday morning,
at an early hour, as I was in my pantry ... the door was suddenly thrown open by a servant, looking wild with excitement, exclaiming, "Oh, madam, do you know?" "Know what,
Henry?" "Alexandria is filled with Yankees." "Are you sure,
Henry?" said I, trembling in every limb. "Sure, madam! I
saw them myself. Before I got up I heard soldiers rushing by
the door; went out, and saw our men going to the cars."
"Did they get off?" I asked, afraid to hear the answer. "Oh,
yes, the cars went off full of them, and some marched out;
and then I went to King Street, and saw such crowds of
Yankees coming in!" ... I lost no time in seeking Mr. Mc-
Guire, who hurried out to hear the truth of the story. ...

The question with us was, what was next to be done? Mr.
McGuire had voted for secession, and there were Union
people enough around us to communicate everything of the
sort to the Federals; and we thought it most prudent to come
off too. Pickets were already thrown out beyond Shuter's
Hill, and they were threatening to arrest all secessionists.

With a heavy heart I packed trunks and boxes, as many as our little carriage would hold.

Chantilly, Virginia. [in the home of a friend] June 6—Mrs. General Lee has been with us for several days. She is on her way to the lower country, and feels that she has left Arlington for an indefinite period. They removed their valuables, silver, etc., but the furniture is left behind. I never saw her more cheerful, and she seems to have no doubt of our success.

June 18—We go today to dine with Bishop Meade. He wishes us to spend much of our time with him. He says he must have the "refugees," as he calls us, at his house. Dear me, I am not yet prepared to think ourselves *refugees,* for I do hope to get home before long. How often do I think of it, as I left it! Not only blooming in its beauty, but the garden filled with vegetables, the strawberries turning on the vines, the young peach-orchard in full bloom; everything teeming with comfort and abundance.

July 18—The soldiers from the far South have never had measles, and most unfortunately it has broken out among them, and many of them have died of it, notwithstanding the attention of surgeons and nurses.

July 23—Before this night is over, loving friends will bear their dead sons home. An express has gone from Winchester to tell them all. They might with truth exclaim, with one of old, whose son was slain, "I would not give my dead son for any living son in Christendom.". . .

Oh, that they would now consent to leave our soil, and return to their own homes! If I know my own heart, I do not desire vengeance upon them, but only that they would leave us in peace, to be forever and forever a separate people.

July 30—News from home. Mr. McD—— says our house has been taken for a hospital, except two or three rooms which are used as headquarters by an officer. . . . The whole neighborhood is one great barracks. . . . Mr. J's and Mr. C's sweet residences have been taken down to the ground to give place for fortifications, which have been thrown up in every direction. Vaucluse, too, the seat of such elegant hospitality, the refined and early-loved home of the F. family, has been levelled to the earth, fortifications thrown up across the lawn, the fine old trees felled, and the whole grounds, once so embowered and shut out from public gaze, now laid bare and open—Vaucluse no more! There seems no probability of our getting home, and if we cannot go, what then? What will become of our furniture, and all our comforts, books, pictures, etc.! . . .

August 20—My old friend, Mrs. D——, has had many trials while in the enemy's lines. Her husband and grown son are in the Confederate service; she has sent her two young daughters to her friends in the lower country, and has remained as the protector of her property, with her two sons of eight and ten, as her companions. . . . A trying scene occurred a short time ago. Our soldiers were surrounding her house, when Colonel Stuart sent off a raiding party. During that night the Yankees advanced, and our men retired. The Yankees at once heard that the raiders were out; but in what direction was the question. They came up to her house, and knowing the mother too well to attempt to extort anything from her, ordered the little boys to tell them in what direction Colonel Stuart had gone. The boys told them that they could tell nothing. Threats followed; finally handcuffs and irons for the ankles were brought. Still those little heroes stood, the one as pale as ashes, the other with his teeth clenched over his under lip, until the blood was ready to gush out, but not one word could be extorted, until, with a feeling of hopelessness in their efforts, they went off, calling them cursed little rebels, etc. The mother saw all this, and stood it unflinchingly—poor thing! . . .

"The Briars," October 2, 1861—Mrs. General Lee has been staying at Annfield, at Media, sick, and without a home. All Virginia has open doors for the family of General Lee; but in her state of health, how dreadful it is to have no certain abiding place.

November 6—Mr. [McGuire] has gone to the prayer-meeting at Millwood, accompanied by Mr. ———; both will cast their votes for Mr. Davis to be President of these Confederate States for the next six years.

January 20, 1862—[A friend of Mrs. McGuire's received word that her son had been seriously wounded and was in a hospital twenty miles from Washington. In trying there to get a passport to visit him, she met a former friend from her home state of Kentucky.]

Next morning, in passing through the parlours [of the hotel], she encountered a lady from her own state, who greeted her pleasantly; she was preparing to entertain her friends— it was New Year's day. "Won't you be with us, Mrs. P.? You may meet some old friends." An apology for declining the invitation was given, by a simple statement of her object in coming to Washington. "Where is your son?" "In the Southern army." "Oh," she exclaimed, "not in the rebel camp! Not a rebel!" and she curled her loyal lip in scorn. "Yes," was the quiet reply, "he is what you call a rebel; but it is the honoured name which Washington bore;" and with a spirit not soothed by her countrywoman, she passed on to the street. . . .

Richmond, February 5—[Mr. McGuire] received a letter, announcing his appointment to a clerkship in the Post-Office Department. The pleasure and gratitude with which it is received is only commensurate with the necessity which made him apply for it. It seems a strange state of things which induces a man, who has ministered and served the altar for thirty-six years, to accept joyfully a situation purely secular, for the sole purpose of making his living; but no chaplaincy could be obtained except on the field, which would neither suit his health, his age, nor his circumstances. His salary will pay his board and mine in Richmond, and the girls will stay in the country until they or I can obtain writing [employment] from Government ... or something else. We are spending a few days with our niece, Mrs. H. A. C., until we can find board. ... Tomorrow I shall go in pursuit of quarters.

February 6—Spent this day in walking from one boarding-house to another, and have returned fatigued and hopeless. I do not believe there is a vacant spot in the city. ...

February 23—The President stood at the base of that noble equestrian statue of Washington, and took the oath which was taken by the "Father of his Country" more than seventy years ago—just after the "great rebellion," in the success of which we all, from Massachusetts to Georgia, so heartily gloried. No wonder that he spoke as if he were inspired.

Last night was the first levee. The rooms were crowded. The President looked weary and grave, but was all suavity and cordiality, and Mrs. Davis won all hearts by her usual unpretending kindness.

March 7—[Mrs. McGuire met in a store a "very plain-looking woman" whose 54-year-old husband was joining the Confederate Army.] "But won't you be very uneasy about him?" I said. "Yes, indeed; but you know he ought to go—them wretches must be drove away." "Did you want your sons to go?" "Want 'em to go!" she exclaimed; "Yes; if they hadn't a-gone, they shouldn't a-staid whar I was. But they wanted to go, *my* sons did." Two days ago, I met her again in a baker's shop; she was filling her basket with cakes and pies. "Well," said I, "has your husband gone?" "No, but he's agwine tomorrow, and I'm getting something for him now."

"Don't you feel sorry as the time approaches for him to go?"
"Oh, yes, I shall miss him mightily; but I ain't never cried
about it; I never shed a tear for the old man, nor for the
boys neither, and I ain't agwine to. Them Yankees must not
come a-nigh to Richmond; if they does, I will fight them
myself. The women must fight, for they *shan't* cross Mayo's
Bridge; they *shan't* git to Richmond." I said to her, "You are
a patriot." "Yes, honey—ain't you? Ain't everybody?" I was
sorry to leave this heroine in homespun, but she was too
busy buying cakes, etc., for the "old man," to be interrupted
any longer.

[Later, in the hospital, she talked about prayer with the
wounded men:] ... "Though I can't bear the Yankees,"
[one of them said] "I believe some of them are Christians, and
pray as hard as we do." "Monstrous few of 'em," grunted out
a man lying near him, "and if we pray for one thing, and they
pray for another, I don't know what to think of our prayers
clashing." "Well, but what do you think of the justice of our
cause? Don't you believe that God will hear us for the
justice of our cause?" "Our cause," he exclaimed, "yes, it is
just; God knows it is just. I never thought of looking at it that
way before, and I was *mighty* uneasy about the Yankee
prayers. I am *mightily obleeged* to you for telling me."

April 10—Spent yesterday in the hospital by the bedside
of Nathan Newton, our little Alabamian. I closed his eyes
last night at ten o'clock, after an illness of six weeks. His
body, by his own request, will be sent to his mother. ... The
packing of his little knapsack reminds me of

THE JACKET OF GRAY

Fold it up carefully, lay it aside,
Tenderly touch it, look on it with pride,
For dear must it be to our hearts evermore,
The jacket of gray, our loved soldier-boy wore. ...

May 2—Our young friend, J. S. M., is here, very ill; I am assisting to nurse him. I feel most anxious about him; he and his four brothers are nobly defending their country. They have strong motives, personal as well as patriotic. Their venerable father and mother, and two young sisters were forced to leave their comfortable home in Fairfax a year ago. The mother has sunk into the grave, an early sacrifice, while the father and sisters continue to be homeless. Their house has been burnt to the ground by Federal soldiers—furniture, clothing, important papers, all consumed. Sad as this story is, it is the history of so many families that it has ceased to call forth remark.

May 13—The croakers roll their gloomy eyes, and say, "Ah, General Jackson is so rash!" and a lady even assured me that he was known to be crazy when under excitement, and that we had everything to fear from the campaign he was now beginning in the Valley. I would that every officer and soldier in the Southern army was crazed in the same way; how soon we would be free from despotism and invasion!

May 14—Even General Lee does not escape animadversion, and the President is the subject of the most bitter maledictions. I have been shocked to hear that a counter-revolution, if not openly advocated, has been distinctly foreshadowed, as the only remedy for our ills.

May 15—It is now ascertained beyond doubt that my nephew, William B. Newton, reported "missing," at Williamsburg, is a prisoner in the enemy's hands. We are very anxious for his exchange, but there seems some difficulty in effecting it. His father, accompanied by Colonel Robertson ... called to see the President a few nights ago, hoping to do something for him. ... In answer to their card, he desired to see the gentlemen in his study, where he was reclining on a sofa, apparently much fatigued, while Mrs. Davis sat at a table engaged in some fine needle-work. The

President immediately arose and received the gentlemen most courteously, introducing them to Mrs. Davis. Colonel Robertson stated the object of the visit . . . and urged the President to use every effort to procure his exchange. The President seemed deeply interested in the subject, and regretted that nothing could then be done, as there was a difficulty pending between the belligerents on the subject of exchange; as soon as that difficulty was removed he would, with pleasure, do all in his power to procure the exchange. Mrs. Davis listened with much interest to the conversation, and her feelings became warmly interested. She said that her husband was a father, and would feel deep sympathy; but if, in the pressure of public business, the subject should pass from his mind, she would certainly remind him of it. She made a very favorable impression on the minds of these gentlemen, who had never seen her before, by her ease of manner, agreeable conversation, and the kindness of heart which she manifested. After a most pleasant interview of an hour, the visitors arose to take leave, but Mrs. Davis invited them with so much cordiality to remain to take a cup of tea with them, which, she said, was then coming up, that they could not decline. The servant brought in the tea-tray, accompanied by some light refreshment. Mrs. Davis poured out the tea for the company of four. The scene reminded them of the unpretending and genial hospitality daily witnessed in the families of Virginia.

May 29— . . . The hospitals in and around Richmond are being cleaned, aired, etc., preparatory to the anticipated battles. Oh, it is sickening to know that these preparations are necessary!

May 31—The booming of cannon, at no very distant point, thrills us with apprehension. We know that a battle is going on. God help us!

June 2—The battle continued yesterday near the field of

the day before. . . . The enemy were repulsed with fearful loss; but our loss was great. The wounded were brought until a late hour last night; and today the hospitals have been crowded with ladies, offering their services to nurse, and the streets are filled with servants darting about, with waiters covered with snowy napkins, carrying refreshments of all kinds to the wounded. Many of the sick, wounded, and weary are in private houses. The roar of the cannon has ceased. . . . Thousands are slain, and yet we seem no nearer the end than when we began! !

June 9, Night— . . . "Thank God," said a man with his leg amputated, "that it was not my right arm, for then I could never have fought again; as soon as this stump is well I shall join Stuart's cavalry; I can ride with a wooden leg as well as a real one."

[In the following selection Mrs. McGuire quoted from her sister's diary "in order that our children's children may know all that our family suffered during this cruel war."]

"27th—Last night I could not sleep, in consequence of the noise made by one of the Yankee soldiers in our kitchen. He said that 30,000 soldiers had been ordered to the Court-House today, to "wipe out" our people. Were our people ignorant of this, and how should we let them know of it? These were questions that haunted me all night. Before day I formed my plan, and awakened S. to consult her on the subject. It was this: To send W. S. [her young son] to the Court-House, *as usual*, for our letters and papers. If the Yankee pickets stopped him, he could return; if he could reach our pickets, he could give the alarm. She agreed to it, and as soon as it was day we aroused the child, communicated to him our plan (for we dared not write), he entered into the spirit of it, and by light he was off. I got up and went down to the yard, for I could not sit still; but what was my consternation, after a short time had elapsed, to see at the gate, and all along the road, the hated red streamers of our enemy going towards the Court-House! S. and myself were miserable about W. [the child]. M. and C. gave us no comfort; they thought it very rash in us to send him—he would be captured, and "Fax" [the horse] would certainly be taken. We told them it was worth the risk to put our people on their guard; but, nevertheless, we were unhappy beyond expression. . . . What was our relief to see W. ride in, escorted by fourteen lancers, he and his horse unmolested! The child had gone ahead of the Yankees, reached our picket, told his story, and a vidette had immediately been sent with the information to headquarters. . . .

"June 1—Dr. N. and Dr. T. have been accused by the Yankees of having informed our people of their meditated attack the other day. They were cross-examined on the subject, and of course denied it positively. They were threatened very harshly, the Yankees contending that there was no one else in the neighborhood that could have done it. Poor little W. was not suspected at all—they little know what women and children can do.

"14th—While quietly sitting on the porch yesterday evening, I saw a young man rapidly approaching the house, on foot; . . . he was one of our soldiers, and from his excited manner there was something unusual the matter. . . . His brother . . . had been killed about two miles from W. The mill-cart from W. soon after passed along, and he put his brother's body into it, and brought it to W. There he found a Yankee picket stationed. C. immediately took the dead soldier into her care, promising to bury him as tenderly as if he were her brother. . . . As soon as we saw him safely off, we rode over to W. to assist in preparing the body for the burial. Oh, what a sad office! . . . He looked so young—not more than twenty years of age. He was shot in four places. . . . We cut a large lock of his hair, as the only thing we could do for his

mother. We have sent for Mr. Carraway to perform the funeral services, and shall bury him by our dear Willie Phelps,
another victim of this unholy war."

[Back to Mrs. McGuire's own diary:]

June 27—The fighting [near Richmond] is even now re-
newed, for I hear the firing of heavy artillery. Last night our
streets were thronged until a late hour to catch the last accounts from couriers and spectators returning from the field.
A bulletin from the Assistant Surgeon of the Fortieth, sent
to his anxious father, assured me of the safety of some of
those most near to me; but the sickening sight of the ambulances bringing in the wounded met my eye at every
turn. The President, and many others, were on the surrounding hills during the night, deeply interested spectators. The
calmness of the people during the progress of the battle was
marvellous. The balloons of the enemy hovering over the
battlefield could be distinctly seen from the outskirts of the
city, and the sound of musketry was distinctly heard. All
were anxious, but none alarmed for the safety of the city.
From the firing of the first gun till the close of the battle
every spot favourable for observation was crowded. The tops
of the Exchange, the Ballard House, the Capitol, and almost
every other tall house were covered with human beings; and
after nightfall the commanding hills from the President's
house to the Alms-House were covered, like a vast amphi-
theatre, with men, women and children, witnessing the
grand display of fireworks—beautiful, yet awful—and sending death amid those whom our hearts hold so dear. I am
told (for I did not witness it) that it was a scene of unsur-
passed magnificence. The brilliant light of bombs bursting
in the air and passing to the ground, the innumerable lesser
lights, emitted by thousands and thousands of muskets, together with the roar of artillery and the rattling of small-
arms, constituted a scene terrifically grand and imposing.

What spell has bound our people? Is their trust in God, and in the valour of our troops, so great that they are unmoved by these terrible demonstrations of our powerful foe? It would seem so, for when the battle was over the crowd dispersed and retired to their respective homes with the seeming tranquility of persons who had been witnessing a panorama of transactions in a far-off country, in which they felt no personal interest; though they knew that their countrymen slept on their arms, only awaiting the dawn to renew the deadly conflict, on the success of which depended not only the fate of our capital, but of that splendid army, containing the material on which our happiness depends.

September 12—Took a ride this evening with Mrs. D. through the beautiful environs of this city. After getting beyond the hospitals, there was nothing to remind us of war; all was peaceful loveliness; we talked of days long past, and almost forgot that our land was the scene of bitter strife. Sometimes I almost fancy that we are taking one of our usual summer trips, with power to return when it terminates; and then I am aroused, as from a sweet dream, to find myself a homeless wanderer, surrounded by horrors of which my wildest fancy had never conceived a possibility, in this Christian land and enlightened day.

September 30—The *Richmond Examiner* of yesterday contains Lincoln's Proclamation, declaring all the Negroes free from the 1st of January next! The abolition papers are in ecstasies; as if they did not know that it can only be carried out *within their* lines. . . .

Richmond, October 15—She [Mrs. McIntosh] dreamed, a few nights after little Jemmie's death, of being at Fort Smith, her home before the war; standing on the balcony of her husband's quarters, her attention was arrested by a procession—an officer's funeral. As it passed under the balcony she called to a passer-by, "Whose funeral is that?" "General

McIntosh's, madam." She was at once aroused, and ran to her sister's room in agony. She did what she could to comfort her, but the dream haunted her imagination. A few days afterwards she saw a servant ride into the yard, with a note for Mrs. K. Though no circumstance was more common, she at once exclaimed, "It is about my husband." She did not know that the battle had taken place; but it was the fatal telegram.

Ashland, October 19—We are now snugly fixed in Ashland. Our mess consists of Bishop J. and family, Major J. and wife, Lieutenant J. J. and wife (our daughter), Mrs. S. and daughter, of Chantilly, Mr. McGuire, myself, and our two young daughters—a goodly number for a cottage with eight small rooms; but we are very comfortable. All from one neighborhood, all refugees, and *none able to do better,* we are determined to take everything cheerfully. Many remarks are jestingly made suggestive of unpleasant collisions among so many families in one house; but we anticipate no evils of that kind; each has her own place, and her own duties to perform; the young married ladies of the establishment are by common consent to have the housekeeping troubles; their husbands are to be masters, with the onerous duties of caterers, treasurers, etc. We old ladies have promised to give our sage advice and experience, whenever it is desired. The girls will assist their sisters, with their nimble fingers, in cases of emergency; and the clerical gentlemen are to have their own way, and to do their work without let or hindrance. . . . With these discreet regulations, we confidently expect a most pleasant and harmonious establishment.

November 29—Luxuries have been given up long ago, by many persons. Coffee is $4 per pound, and good tea from $18 to $20; butter ranges from $1.50 to $2 per pound; lard 50 cents; corn $15 per barrel; and wheat $4.50 per bushel. We can't get a muslin dress for less than $6 or $8 per yard; calico

$1.75, etc. This last is no great hardship, for we will all resort to homespun. We are knitting our own stockings, and regret that we did not learn to spin and weave. The North Carolina homespun is exceedingly pretty, and makes a genteel dress.

December 15—An exciting day. Trains have been constantly passing with the wounded for the Richmond hospitals. Every lady, every child, every servant in the village, has been engaged preparing and carrying food to the wounded as the cars stopped at the depot—coffee, tea, soup, milk, and everything we could obtain. With eager eyes and beating hearts we watched for those most dear to us. Sometimes they were so slightly injured as to sit at the windows and answer our questions, which they were eager to do. They exult in the victory. I saw several poor fellows shot through the mouth—they only wanted milk; it was soothing and cooling to their lacerated flesh. One, whom I did not see, had both eyes shot out. But I cannot write of the horrors of this day. Nothing but an undying effort to administer to their comfort could have kept us up. The gratitude of those who were able to express it was so touching! They said that the ladies were at every depot with refreshments. As the cars would move off, those who were able would *shout* their blessings on the ladies of Virginia: "We will fight, we will protect the ladies of Virginia." Ah, poor fellows, what can the ladies of Virginia ever do to compensate them for all they have done and suffered for us? As a train approached late this evening, we saw comparatively few sitting up. It was immediately surmised that it contained the desperately wounded—perhaps many of the dead. With eager eyes we watched, and before it stopped I saw Surgeon J. P. Smith (my connection) spring from the platform, and come towards me; my heart stood still. "What is it, Doctor? Tell me at once." "Your nephews, Major B. and Captain C., are both on the train, dangerously wounded." "Mortally?"

"We hope not. You will not be allowed to enter the car; come to Richmond tomorrow morning; B. will be there for you to nurse. I shall carry W. C. on the morning cars to his mother at the University. We will do our best for both."

February 26, 1863—The papers are full of the probable, or rather *hoped for*, intervention of France. The proposition of the Emperor, contained in a letter from the minister to Seward, and his artful, wily, Seward-like reply, are in a late paper. We pause to see what will be the next step of the Emperor. Oh that he would recognize us, and let fanatical England pursue her own cold, selfish course!

March 5—Several of us are engaged in making soap, and selling it, to buy things which seem essential to our wardrobes. A lady who has been perfectly independent in her circumstances, finding it necessary to do something of the kind for her support, has been very successful in making pickles and catsups for the restaurants. Another, like Mrs. Primrose, rejoices in her success in making gooseberry wine which sparkles like champagne, and is the best domestic wine I ever drank; this is designed for the highest bidder. . . . A gentleman, lately from Columbia, tells me that the South Carolina girls pride themselves on their palmetto hats; and the belle of a large fortune, who used to think no bonnet presentable but one made by the first New York or Parisian milliner, now glories in her palmetto. . . .

The *poor*, being well supplied with Government work, are better off than usual.

March 15—Our dear friend Mrs. S. has just heard of the burning of her house at beautiful Chantilly. The Yankee officers had occupied it as headquarters, and on leaving it, set fire to every house on the land, except the overseer's house and one of the servants' quarters. Such ruthless vandalism do they commit wherever they go! I expressed my surprise to Mrs. S. that she was enabled to bear it so well. She calmly replied, "God has spared my sons through so many battles, that I should be ungrateful indeed to complain of anything else." This lovely spot has been her home from her marriage, and the native place of her many children, and when I remember it as I saw it two years ago, I feel that it is too hard for her to be thus deprived of it. An officer [Federal] quartered there last winter, describing it in a letter to the *New York Herald,* says the furniture had been "removed," except a large old-fashioned sideboard; he had been indulging his curiosity by reading the many private letters which he found scattered about the house; some of which, he says, were written by General Washington, "with whom the family seem to have been connected."

April 2—We were shocked when the gentlemen returned, to hear of the riot which occurred in Richmond today. A mob, principally of women, appeared in the streets, attacking the stores. Their object seemed to be to get anything they could; dry-goods, shoes, brooms, meat, glassware, jewelry, were caught up by them. The military was called out—the Governor dispersed them from one part of town, telling them that unless they disappeared in five minutes, the soldiers should fire among them. This he said, holding his watch in his hand. . . . It is the first time that such a thing has ever darkened the annals of Richmond. God grant it may be the last.

April 18—A letter from our son J. today; full of pleasant feeling at finding himself again in the Army of Northern Virginia. He is just established near General Jackson's headquarters, as Surgeon of the First Virginia Battalion; had just breakfasted with Stonewall, and is filled with enthusiastic admiration for the great Christian soldier and patriot.

May 12—How can I record the sorrow which has befallen our country! General T. J. Jackson is no more. The good, the great, the glorious Stonewall Jackson is numbered with the dead! . . . Perhaps we have trusted too much to an arm of flesh; for he was the nation's idol. His soldiers almost worshipped him, and it may be that God has therefore removed him. We bow in meek submission to the great Ruler of events.

May 16—I have been in Richmond for two days past, nursing the wounded of our little hospital. Some of them are very severely injured, yet they are the most cheerful invalids I ever saw. It is remarked in all the hospitals that the cheerfulness of the wounded in proportion to their suffering is much greater than that of the sick. Under my care, yesterday, was one poor fellow, with a ball embedded in his neck; another with an amputated leg; one with a hole in his breast, through which a bullet had passed; another with a shattered arm; and others with slighter wounds; yet all showed indomitable spirit; evinced a readiness to be amused or interested in everything around them; asked that the morning papers might be read to them, and gloried in their late victory; and expressed an anxiety to get well, that they may have another *"chance at them fellows."*

May 18—This morning we had the gratification of a short visit from General Lee. He called and breakfasted with us, while the other passengers in the cars breakfasted at the hotel. We were very glad to see that great and good man look so well and so cheerful. His beard is very long, and painfully gray, which makes him appear much older than he really is. One of the ladies at table, with whom he is closely connected, rallied him on allowing his beard to grow, saying, "Cousin Robert, it makes you look too venerable for your years." He was amused, and pleaded as his excuse the inconvenience of shaving in camp. "Well," she replied, "if I were in Cousin Mary's place [Mrs. Lee's] I would allow it to remain now, but I would take it off as soon as the war is over." He answered, while a shade passed over his bright countenance, "When the war is over, my dear L., she may take my beard off, and my head with it, if she chooses." This he said as the whistle summoned him to his seat in the cars, not meaning to depress us, or imagining for an instant that we would think of it again; but it proved to us that he *knew* that the end was not yet, and disappointed us, for after every great victory we cannot help hoping that the Federal government may be tired of war and bloodshed, rapine and murder, and withdraw its myriads to more innocent pursuits.

Wednesday [June, 1863]—I don't want their women and children to suffer; nor that our men should follow their example, and break through and steal. I want our warfare carried on in a more honourable way; but I do want our men and horses to be fed on the good things of Pennsylvania; I want the fine dairies, pantries, granaries, meadows and orchards belonging to the rich farmers of Pennsylvania, to be laid open to our army; and I want it all paid for with our *Confederate money, which will be good at some future day.*

June 6— ... Our old friend, Mrs. T., of Rappahannock County ... gives most graphic descriptions of her sojourn of seven weeks among the Yankees last summer. Sixty thousand surrounded her house, under command of General Siegel. On one occasion, he and his staff rode up and announced that they would *take tea with her.* Entirely alone, that elegant old lady retained her composure, and with unruffled countenance rang her bell; when the servant appeared, she said to him, "John, tea for fourteen." She quietly retained her seat, conversing with them with dignified politeness, and submitting as best she could to the General's very free manner of walking about her beautiful establishment pronouncing it "baronial," and regretting, in her presence, that he had not known of its elegancies and comforts in time, that he might have brought on Mrs. Siegel, and have made it his headquarters. Tea being announced, Mrs. T., before proceeding to the dining-room, requested the servant to call a soldier in, who had been guarding her house for weeks, and who had sought occasion to do her many kindnesses. When the man entered, the General demurred: "No, no, madam, he will not go to table with us." Mrs. T. replied, "General, I must beg that you will allow this *gentleman* to come to *my table*, for *he* has been a friend to me when I have sadly wanted one." The General objected no farther; the *man* took tea with the master. After tea, the General proposed music, asking Mrs. T. if she had ever played; she replied that "such was still her habit." The piano being opened, she said if she sang at all she must sing the songs of her own land, and then, with her uncommonly fine voice, she sang "The Bonnie Blue Flag," "Dixie," and other Southern songs with great spirit. They listened with apparent pleasure. One of the staff then suggested that the General was a musician. Upon her vacating the seat he took it, and played in grand style, with so much beauty and accuracy, she added, with a twinkle of her eye, that "I strongly suspected him of having been a music-master."

July 3—Our troops seem to be walking over Pennsylvania without let or hindrance. They have taken possession of Chambersburg, Carlisle, and other smaller towns. They surrendered without firing a gun. I am glad to see that General Lee orders his soldiers to respect private property; but it will be difficult to make an incensed soldiery, whose houses have in many instances been burned, crops wantonly destroyed, horses stolen, Negroes persuaded off, hogs and sheep shot down and left in the field in warm weather—it will be difficult to make such sufferers remember the Christian precept of returning good for evil.

July 11—Vicksburg was surrendered on the 4th of July.

The terms of capitulation seem marvellously generous for such a foe. What can the meaning be?

July 19—... We have had this week a visit of two days from Mrs. General Lee. She was on her way to the Hot Springs in pursuit of health, of which she stands greatly in need. She is a great sufferer from rheumatism, but is cheerful, notwithstanding her sufferings, bodily and mentally. She is, of course, unhappy about her imprisoned son, and, I should suppose, about the overpowering responsibilities of her noble husband; but of that you never hear a word from her. She left us this morning, in a box car, fitted up to suit an invalid, with a bed, chairs, etc. She was accompanied by the lovely wife of her captive son, also travelling in pursuit of health. Greater beauty and sweetness rarely fall to the lot of woman; and as I looked at the sad, delicate lineaments of her young face, I could but inwardly pray that the terrible threats denounced against her husband by Yankee authority might never reach her ear; for, though we do not believe that they will dare to offer him violence, yet the mere suggestion would be enough to make her very miserable.

August 10—... That young soldier, the son of a neighbor, related to me an anecdote, some weeks ago... which showed the horrors of this fratricidal war. He said that the day after a battle in Missouri in the fall of 1861, he, among others, was detailed to bury the dead. Some Yankee soldiers were on the field doing the same thing. As they turned over a dead man, he saw a Yankee stop, look intently, and then run to the spot with an exclamation of horror. In a moment he was on his knees by the body, in a paroxysm of grief. It was his brother. They were Missourians. The brother now dead had emigrated South some years before. He said that before the war communication had been kept up between them, and he had strongly suspected that he was in the army; he had consequently been in constant search of his brother. The Northern and Southern soldiers then united in burying him, who was brother in arms of the one, and the mother's son of the other!

November 11—Just received a visit from my nephew, W. N., who is on his way to Fauquier to be married. I had not seen him since he lost his leg. He is still on crutches, and it made my heart bleed to see him walk with such difficulty. I believe that neither war, pestilence, nor famine could put an end to the marrying and giving in marriage which is constantly going on.

December 13—My appointment to a clerkship in the Commissary Department has been received, with a salary of $125 per month. The rooms are not ready for us to begin our duties, and Colonel R. has just called to tell me one of the requirements. As our duties are those of accountants, we are to go through a formal examination in arithmetic. If we do not, as the University boys say, "pass," we are considered incompetent, and of course are dropped from the list of appointees. This requirement may be right, but it certainly seems to me both provoking and absurd that I must be examined in arithmetic by a commissary major young enough to be my son.

January 1, 1864— ... In all the broad South there will be scarcely a fold without its missing lamb, a fireside without its vacant chair.

March 20—The Transportation Office is just opposite to us, where crowds of furloughed soldiers, returning to their commands are constantly standing waiting for transportation. As I pass them on my way to the office in the morning, I always stop to have a cheerful word with them. Yesterday morning I said to them: "Gentlemen, whom do you suppose I have seen this morning?" In answer to their inquiring looks, I said: "General Lee." "General Lee," they exclaimed: "I did not know he was in town; God bless him!" and they looked excited, as if they were about to burst forth with "Hurrah for General Lee!" "And where do you suppose I saw him so early?" "Where, Madam—where?" "At prayer-meeting, down upon his knees, praying for you and the country."

July 24—Amid all the turbulent scenes which surround us, our only grandchild has first seen the light, and the dear little fellow looks as quiet as though all were peace. We thank God for this precious gift, this little object of all-absorbing interest, which so pleasantly diverts our troubled minds. . . .

August 12—Some amusing incidents sometimes occur, showing the eagerness of the ladies to serve our troops after a long separation. A lady living near Berryville, but a little remote from the main road, says that when our troops are passing through the country, she sometimes feels sick with anxiety to do something for them. She, one morning, stood in her porch, and could see them turn in crowds to neighbouring houses which happened to be on the road, but no one turned out of the way far enough to come to her house. At last one man came along, and finding that he was passing her gate, she ran out with the greatest alacrity to invite him to come in to get his breakfast. He turned to her with an amused expression and replied: "I am much obliged to you, madam; I wish I could breakfast with you, but as I have already eaten *four* breakfasts to please the ladies, I must beg you to excuse me."

August 22—Just been on a shopping expedition for my sister and niece, and spent $1,500 in about an hour. I gave $110 for ladies' morocco boots; $22 per yard for linen; $5 apiece for spools of cotton; $5 for a paper of pins, etc. It would be utterly absurd, except that it is melancholy, to see our currency depreciating so rapidly.

August 31—Letters from our friends in the Valley, describing the horrors now going on there. A relative witnessed the burning of three very large residences on the 20th of August. ... Two companies of the 5th Michigan Cavalry, commanded by Captain Drake, executed the fearful order. They drew up in front of Mr. ———'s house and asked for him. "Are you Mr. ———?" demanded the Captain. "I have orders to burn your house." In vain Mr. ——— remonstrated. He begged for one hour. ... With a look of hardened ferocity [Captain Drake] turned to the soldiers, with the order: "Men, to your work, and do it thoroughly!" In an instant the torch was applied to that home of domestic elegance and comfort. ... They allowed the family to save as much furniture as they could, but the servants were all gone, and there was no one near to help them. ... Matches were applied to window and bed curtains; burning coals were sprinkled in the linen-closet, containing every variety of house and table linen. Mrs. ———, the daughter, opened a drawer, and taking her jewelry, embracing an elegant diamond ring and other valuables, was escaping with them to the yard, when she was seized by two ruffians on the stair-steps, held by the arms by one, while the other forcibly took the jewels; they then, as she is a very small woman, lifted her over the banister and let her drop into the passage below; fortunately it was not very far and she was not at all injured. ... Mrs. ——— is the only daughter of Mr. ———, and was the only lady on the spot. Her first care, when she found the house burning, was to secure her baby, which was sleeping in its cradle upstairs. A guard was at the foot of the steps, and refused to let her pass; she told him that she was going to rescue her child and did. His bayonet could not stop her; she ran by, and soon returned, bearing her child to a place of safety. When the house had become a heap of ruins, the mother returned from the bedside of her dead sister, whither she had gone at daylight that morning, on horseback. . . . She was, of course, overwhelmed with grief and with horror at the scene before her. As soon as she dismounted, a soldier leaped on the horse, and rode off with it.

Their work of destruction in one place being now over, they left it for another scene of vengeance. The same ceremony of Captain Drake's announcing his orders to the mistress of the mansion . . . being over, the torch was applied. The men had dismounted; the work of pillage was going on merrily; the house was burning in every part, to insure total destruction. The hurried tramp of horses' feet could not be heard amidst the crackling of flames and falling of rafters, but the sudden shout and cry of "No quarter! no quarter!" from many voices, resounded in the ears of the unsuspecting marauders as a death-knell. A company of Mosby's men rushed up the hill and charged them furiously; they were aroused by the sound of danger, and fled hither and thither. Terrified and helpless, they were utterly unprepared for resistance. The cry of "no quarter! no quarter!" still continued. They hid behind the burning ruins; they crouched in the corners of fences; they begged for life; but their day of grace was past. The defenseless women, children, and old men of the neighborhood had borne their tortures too long; something must be done, and all that this one company of braves could do, was done. Thirty were killed on the spot, and others, wounded and bleeding, sought refuge, and asked pity of those whom they were endeavoring to ruin. ———— writes: "Two came to us, the most pitiable objects you ever beheld, and we did what we could for them; for, after all, the men are not to blame half so much as the officers."

September 10—Were I a credulous woman, and ready to

believe all that I hear in the office, in the hospital, in my visits and on the streets, I should think that Richmond is now filled with the most accomplished military geniuses on which the sun shines. Each man expresses himself, as an old friend would say, with the most "dogmatic infallibility" of the conduct of the President, General Lee, General Johnston, General Hampton, General Beauregard, General Wise, together with all the other lights of every degree. . . . I would that all such men could be sent to the field; I think at least a regiment could be spared from Richmond, for then the women of the city at least would be more peaceful.

September 16—My brother has lately had a visit from a very interesting young South Carolinian, who came to look for the body of his brother. The two brothers were being educated in Germany when the war broke out; and as soon as they were of military age, with the consent of their parents, they hastened home to take part in their country's struggle. In one of the cavalry fights in Hanover, in May last, one brother was killed, and the other, "not being able to find the body at the time, was now seeking it.". . . He had heard that some of the fallen had been buried at S. H. or W. . . . It was then remembered that there were three graves on the opposite side of the Pamunky River, and one was marked with the name "Tingle." . . . Dr. B. and the brother set out upon their melancholy mission, having obtained a cart, one or two men, and given an order at a neighboring carpenter's shop for a coffin. After crossing the river they found the three graves, at the place designated, in the county of King William. The one marked "Tingle" contained the body of a Federal and one of a Confederate soldier, but not the brother. The next one opened was not the right one; but the third contained the much-loved remains, which were easily recognized by the anxious brother. Tenderly and gently, all wrapped in his blanket, he was transferred from his shallow grave to his soldier's coffin, and then conveyed to S. H. . . . It was now night, the moon shone brightly, and all was ready. The families from both houses gathered around the grave. . . . Mrs. N——, who, with a clear calm voice read by the light of a single lantern the beautiful ritual of the Episcopal Church.

December 26—The sad Christmas has passed away. J. and C. were with us, and very cheerful. We exerted ourselves to be so too. The church services in the morning were sweet and comforting. St. Paul's was dressed most elaborately and beautifully with evergreens; all looked as usual; but there is much sadness on account of the failure of the South to keep Sherman back. When we got home our family circle was small, but pleasant. The Christmas turkey and ham were not. We had aspired to a turkey, but finding the prices range from $50 to $100 in the market on Saturday, we contented ourselves with roast-beef and the various little dishes which Confederate times have made us believe are tolerable substitutes for the viands of better days. At night I treated our little party to tea and ginger cakes—two very rare indulgences; and but for the sorghum, grown in our own fields, the cakes would be an impossible indulgence. Nothing but the well-ascertained fact that Christmas comes but once a year would make such extravagance at all excusable. . . . Two meals a day has become the universal system among refugees, and many citizens, from necessity. . . . A country lady . . . could scarcely believe me when I told her that we had not had milk more than twice in eighteen months, and then it was sent by a country friend. It is now $4 a quart.

January 8, 1865—Some persons in this beleaguered city seem crazed on the subject of gayety. In the midst of the wounded and dying, the low state of the commissariat, the anxiety of the whole country, I am mortified to say that there are gay parties given in the city. There are those denominated "starvation parties," where young persons meet for innocent enjoyment, and retire at a reasonable hour; but there are others where the most elegant suppers are served— cakes, jellies, ices in profusion, and meats of the finest kinds in abundance, such as might furnish a meal for a regiment of General Lee's army. . . .

There seems to be a perfect mania on the subject of matrimony. Some of the churches may be seen open and lighted almost every night for bridals, and wherever I turn I hear of marriages in prospect.

> In peace Love tunes the shepherd's reed;
> In war he mounts the warrior's steed,

sings the "Last Minstrel" of the Scottish days of romance; and I do not think that our modern warriors are a whit behind them either in love or war. My only wonder is, that they find the time for love-making amid the storms of warfare. . . . A soldier in our hospital called to me as I passed his bed the other day, "I say, Mrs. McGuire, when do you think my wound will be well enough for me to go to the country?" "Before very long, I hope." "But what does the doctor say, for I am mighty anxious to go?" I looked at his disabled limb, and talked to him hopefully of his being able to enjoy country air in a short time. "Well, try to get me up, for, you see, it ain't the country air I am after, but I wants to get married, and the lady don't know that I am wounded, and maybe she'll think I don't want to come." "Ah," said I, "but you must show her your scars, and if she is a girl worth having she will love you all the better for having bled for your country; and you must tell her that

It is always the heart that is bravest in war,
That is fondest and truest in love."

He looked perfectly delighted with the idea. . . .

March 10—Still we go on as heretofore, hoping and praying that Richmond may be safe. . . . I know that we ought to feel that whatever General Lee and the President deem right for the cause must be right, and that we should be satisfied that all will be well; but it would almost break my heart to see this dear old city, with its hallowed associations, given over to the Federals.

March 11—Fighting is still going on; so near the city, that the sound of cannon is ever in our ears. Farmers are sending in produce which they cannot spare, but which they give with a spirit of self-denial rarely equalled. Ladies are offering their jewelry, their plate, anything which can be converted into money, for the country. I have heard some of them declare, that, if necessary, they will cut off their long suits of hair, and send them to Paris to be sold for bread for the soldiers; and there is not a woman, worthy of the name of Southerner, who would not do it, if we could get it out of the country, and bread or meat in return. . . .

March 31—A long pause in my diary. Everything seems so dark and uncertain that I have no heart for keeping records. The croakers croak about Richmond being evacuated, but I can't and won't believe it.

April 3—We have passed through a fatal thirty-six hours. Yesterday morning (it seems a week ago) we went, as usual, to St. James's Church. . . . The day was bright, beautiful, and peaceful, and a general quietness and repose seemed to rest upon the congregation, undisturbed by rumours and apprehensions. While the sacred elements were being administered, the sexton came in with a note to General Cooper, which was handed him as he walked from the chancel, and he immediately left the church. It made me anxious; but such things are not uncommon, and caused no excitement in the congregation. The services being over, we left the church, and as the congregations from the various churches were being mingled on Grace Street, our children, who had been at St. Paul's, joined us, on their way to the usual family gathering in our room on Sunday. After the salutations of the morning, J. remarked, in an agitated voice, to his father, that he had just returned from the War Department, and that there was sad news—General Lee's lines had been broken, and the city would probably be evacuated within twenty-four hours. Not until then did I observe that every countenance was wild with excitement. The inquiry, "What is the matter?" ran from lip to lip. Nobody seemed to hear or answer. An old friend ran across the street, pale with excitement, repeating what J. had just told us, that unless we heard better news from General Lee the city would be evacuated. We could do nothing; no one suggested anything to be done. We reached home with a strange, unrealistic feeling. . . . Baggage-wagons, carts, drays, and ambulances were driving about the streets; everyone was going off that could go, and now there were all the indications of alarm and excitement of every kind which could attend such an awful scene. The people were rushing up and down the streets, vehicles of all kinds were flying along, bearing goods of all sorts and people of all ages and classes who could go beyond the corporation lines. . . . Union men began to show themselves; treason walked abroad. A gloomy pall seemed to hang over us; but I do not think that any of us felt keenly, or have yet realized our overwhelming calamity. The suddenness and extent of it is too great for us to feel its poignancy at once. About two o'clock in the morning we were startled by a loud sound like thunder; the house shook and the windows rattled; it seemed like an earthquake in our midst.

We knew not what it was, nor did we care. It was soon understood to be the blowing up of a magazine below the city. . . . The lower part of the city was burning. About seven o'clock I set off to go to the central depot to see if the cars would go out. As I went from Franklin to Broad Street, and on Broad, the pavements were covered with broken glass; women, both white and coloured, were walking in multitudes from the Commissary offices and burning stores with bags of flour, meal, coffee, sugar, rolls of cotton cloth, etc.; coloured men were rolling wheelbarrows filled in the same way. I went on and on towards the depot, and as I proceeded shouts and screams became louder. The rabble rushed by me in one stream. At last I exclaimed, "Who are those shouting? What is the matter?" I seemed to be answered by a hundred voices, "The Yankees have come." I turned to come home, but what was my horror, when I reached Ninth Street, to see a regiment of Yankee cavalry come dashing up, yelling, shouting, hallooing, screaming! All Bedlam let loose could not have vied with them in diabolical roarings. I stood riveted to the spot; I could not move nor speak. Then I saw the iron gates of our time-honoured and beautiful Capitol Square, on the walks and greensward of which no hoof had been allowed to tread, thrown open and the cavalry dash in. I could see no more; I must go on with a mighty effort, or faint where I stood. . . . The Federal soldiers were roaming about the streets; either whiskey or the excess of joy had given some of them the appearance of being beside themselves. . . . It soon became evident that protection would be necessary for the residences, and at the request of Colonel P. I went to the Provost Marshall's office to ask for it. . . . Only ladies were allowed to apply for guards. Of course this was a very unpleasant duty, but I must undertake it. Mrs. D. agreed to accompany me, and we proceeded to the City Hall —the City Hall, which from my childhood I had regarded with respect and reverence, as the place where my father had for years held his courts, and in which our lawyers, whose names stand among the highest in the Temple of Fame, for fifty years expounded the Constitution and the laws, which must now be trodden under foot. . . . We passed the sentinel, and an officer escorted us to the room in which we were to ask our country's foe to allow us to remain undisturbed in our own houses. Mrs. D. leant on me tremblingly; she shrank from the humiliating duty. For my own part, though my heart beat loudly and my blood boiled, I never felt more high-spirited or lofty than at that moment. A large table was surrounded by officials, writing or talking to the ladies, who came on the same mission that brought us. I approached the officer who sat at the head of the table, and asked him politely if he was the Provost Marshal. "I am the Commandant, madam," was the respectful reply. "Then to whom am I to apply for protection for our residence?" "You need none, madam; our troops are perfectly disciplined, and dare not enter your premises." "I am sorry to be obliged to undeceive you, sir, but when I left home seven of your soldiers were in the yard of the residence opposite to us, and one has already been into our kitchen." He looked surprised, and said, "Then, madam, you are entitled to a guard. Captain, write a protection for the residence on the corner of First and Franklin Streets, and give these ladies a guard.". . . Mrs. D. and myself came out, accompanied by our guard. The fire was progressing rapidly, and the crashing sound of falling timbers was distinctly heard. Dr. Read's church was blazing. Yankees, citizens, and Negroes were attempting to arrest the flames. The War Department was falling in; burning papers were being wafted about the streets. . . . We brought our guard to Colonel P., who posted him; about three o'clock he came to tell me that the guard was drunk, and threatening to shoot the servants in the yard. Again I went to City

Hall to procure another. . . . Almost every house is guarded; and the streets are now (ten o'clock) perfectly quiet. The moon is shining brightly on our captivity. God guide and watch over us!

April 5—I feel as if we were groping in the dark; no one knows what to do. The Yankees, so far, have behaved humanely. As usual, they begin with professions of kindness to those whom they have ruined without justifiable cause, without reasonable motive, without right to be here or anywhere else within the Southern boundary. General Ord is said to be polite and gentlemanly, and seems to do everything in his power to lessen the horrors of this dire calamity.

April 6—Mr. Lincoln has visited our devoted city today. His reception was anything but complimentary. Our people were in nothing rude or disrespectful; they only kept themselves away from a scene so painful.

April 10—Another gloomy Sabbath-day and harrowing night. We went to St. Paul's in the morning. . . . I could not listen; I felt so strangely, as if in a vivid, horrible dream. Neither President was prayed for; in compliance with some arrangement with the Federal authorities, the prayer was used as for all in authority! How fervently did we all pray for our own President! Thank God, our silent prayers are free from Federal authority.

Thursday Night [April 13]—Fearful rumours are reaching us from sources which it is hard to doubt, that it is all too true, and that General Lee surrendered on Sunday last, the 9th of April. The news came to the enemy by telegram during the day, and to us at night by the hoarse and pitiless voice of the cannon. We know, of course, that circumstances forced it upon our great commander and his gallant army. How all this happened—how Grant's hundreds of thousands overcame our little band, history, not I, must tell my children's children.

Sunday Night [April 16]—General Lee has returned. He came unattended, save by his staff—came without notice, and without parade; but he could not come unobserved; as soon as his approach was whispered, a crowd gathered in his path, not boisterously, but respectfully, and increasing rapidly as he advanced to his home on Franklin Street, between 8th and 9th, where, with a courtly bow to the multitude, he at once retired to the bosom of his beloved family. When I called in to see his high-minded and patriotic wife, a day or two after the evacuation, she was busily engaged in her invalid's chair, and very cheerful and hopeful. "The end is not yet," she said, as if to cheer those around her; "Richmond is not the Confederacy."

Tuesday Night [April 18]—Our country relatives have been very kind. My brother offers us an asylum in his devastated home at W. While there we must look around for some other place, in which to build a home for our declining years. Property we have none—all gone. Thank God, we have our faculties; the girls and myself, at least, have health. Mr. McGuire bears up under our difficulties with the same hopeful spirit which he has ever manifested. "The Lord will provide," is still his answer to any doubts on our part. The Northern officials offer free tickets to persons returning to their homes—alas! to their *homes!* How few of us have homes. Some are confiscated; others destroyed. The families of the army and navy officers are here.

April 20—A whole-hearted friend from Alexandria met me the other day and with the straightforward simplicity due to friendship in these trying times, asked me at once, "Has your husband any money?" I told him I thought not. He replied, "Tell him I have between twenty-five and thirty dollars—that's all—and he shall have half of it; tell him I say so."

April 24—On Saturday evening my brother's wagon met

us at the depot and brought us to this place, beautiful in its ruins. . . . We miss the respectful and respectable servants, born in the family and brought up with an affection for the household which seemed a part of their nature, and which so largely contributed to the happiness both of master and servant. Even the nurse of our precious little J., the sole child of the house . . . has gone. It is touching to hear the sweet child's account of the shock she experienced when she found that her "mammy," deceived and misled by the minions who followed Grant's army, had left her. . . .

May 4—General Johnston surrendered on the 26th of April. "My native land, good-night."

CHAPTER NINE

Slaves Cheered and Helped Their Masters

ONLY A SOUTHERNER CAN FULLY UNDERSTAND A DEVOTION *between master and slave so deep that a slave often accompanied his master to battle to serve and protect him—in spite of the fact that the master was at war to keep the slave in bondage. This incredible relationship did exist, however, as Southerners know. Some masters, of course, took their slaves with them when they went to war, giving them no choice in the matter. But many accompanied their masters of their own free wills. For example, Mrs. John E. Golden of Bowie County, Texas, tells:*

My mother's eldest brother, Dr. William Sparkman, made ready to leave for Richmond immediately upon word that South Carolina had seceded. Anthony, my grandfather's "head man," had cared for "Marse William" all his life and would not consent for him to go alone. Persuasion did no good, so in the long run another horse was saddled and brought out for Anthony, and to Richmond he also went. Through the grapevine he heard of the battles back home in Mississippi and the raids being made and of the destruction in many places, so his thoughts turned back to his "white folks" and he decided to return to his Missus—he must warn them and take care of them. Anthony, slipping through the lines, maneuvering day and night, frantically worked his way a little ahead. When at last he arrived, ragged and tired, he did not stop until he had emptied the smokehouse of all meat, lard, etc.; took it to the swamp and hid and buried it so that neither Yankees nor beasts found or molested it.

Mrs. Hunter C. Bourne of Hanover County, Virginia, tells another story of a slave who went off to battle with his master and later had to deliver sad news to his "white folks" at home:

On an evening following one of the battles of the Wilderness in 1864, the Negro boy who had accompanied Dr. Joe Baker to war came to the Baker house to tell them that Dr. Joe was reported missing. . . . This slave like so many of the faithful colored folks, had gone to war to look after his young master. It was decided that fourteen-year-old Ellis Baker should go to search for his brother, Dr. Joe. Ellis and the colored boy got on an old mule left by the Yankees and with a farm lantern set out for the battlefield. With the light of the lantern the boys searched among the dead and wounded for Dr. Joe.

The pitiful cries for water from the wounded caused the boys to take canteens from the bodies of those beyond such needs and give them to the living. After a time they realized that if they kept stopping they could cover little ground, so steeling themselves, they continued only to search—turning bodies over here and there so that the lantern could cast its light on faces. After hours they found Dr. Joe—unconscious but still alive. The boys got him across the old mule and made their way home. In spite of severe wounds Dr. Joe was nursed back to health and returned to the army before the close of the war.

Many may have over-sentimentalized the relationship be-tween slaves and their white families, but it is nevertheless a fact that at the outbreak of war large numbers of slaves felt complete loyalty to the South. Mrs. Alice Lee Humphreys of Anderson County, South Carolina, says she still feels a lump in her throat when she remembers this evidence of a slave's devotion to her mistress.

The principals of this story were my grandmother, her small Negro slave girl, and a group of Yankee marauders. When news reached her plantation near Anderson, South Carolina, that the Union soldiers were near, my grandmother sent the horses and other livestock by Negro slaves to a wooded area for safe keeping. Then she hid her silver under the smokehouse and sat down with her knitting and what composure she could muster to await the invaders. By her side crouched Dilcey, an alert little Negro girl, now wide-eyed and terrified.

"Get up, Dilcey," ordered my grandmother. "Get busy at something. We must not let them know we are afraid!"

Small Dilcey grabbed a cloth and began dusting obediently. It was then that Grandmother, glancing up, saw her prized gold watch on its nail by the mantel. But it was too late. Already, the intruders were there!

The Yankees made a thorough search of the room, then by a back stairway went to the second floor. The two frightened listeners heard a terrific pounding of boots overhead.

After what seemed an eternity, the raiding party left the house. My grandmother looked up apprehensively at the nail by the mantel. The watch was gone!

"They got my watch, Dilcey," she began heatedly.

Dilcey came forward. She thrust her small black hand into her bosom, and brought out the dust cloth. In its folds lay something that gleamed in the afternoon light.

"No Yankee mens is goin' to git my Mistis's watch!" she said with simple, but stubborn loyalty.

Some slaves proved their loyalty to their white masters in the most tangible of all ways: they risked or gave their lives rather than betray their masters. The following true stories illustrate such selfless devotion:

When the Yankee soldiers reached my grandfather's plantation they took the slave who had helped hide his valuables and knew where everything was and tried to make him tell on his master. But he would tell them nothing. They took him to the front yard, made him lie down on the ground, held the muzzle of a gun to his mouth, and told him they would shoot if he did not talk. He still refused to betray his master, and the soldiers let him go unharmed. The soldiers never found the treasure.

In front of Hopewell Associated Reformed Presbyterian Church in Chester, South Carolina, is a memorial stone for Burwell Hemphill. He was a slave of Robert Hemphill, a member of Hopewell Church. Indeed both master and slave were members of this church. The stone commemorates the fact that Burwell, the slave, was hung by Sherman's raiders when they passed through this section. The raiders tried to make Burwell reveal the hiding place of his master's valuables. They swung him up several times, then would lower him down, and would try each time to make him tell where he had hidden those things. Truly he gave his life for his master. He died rather than be unfaithful to those he loved and served.

Some slaves wanted their freedom; others did not. Here are two contrasting examples of the feelings of the slaves themselves on the controversial subject of emancipation. The first was described in a letter to the folks back home written by a private in the 18th Regiment of Massachusetts Volunteers:

Before I came here, I was often told that I should not think so badly of slavery if I had been in the slave states. But I must say I have not yet seen any beauty in the system. While on picket duty I often meet with slaves and have opportunities of conversing with them. I said to one who came into the camp the other day, "How have you been treated, Robert?" "Pretty well, sar." "Have you been well fed and clothed?" "Pretty well till dis year. Massa hab no money to spare dis year." "Were you contented?" "No, sar." "You say you were pretty well treated and pretty well supplied with food and clothes; why weren't you contented then?" "Cause I wanted to be free, sar." "But what could you do to support yourself and your wife and children if you were all free?" His face brightened and you could see his eyes sparkle as he replied, "I'd hire a little hut and hab a little garden and keep a pig and a cow, and I'd work out by the day and save money. I *could* save money. I've laid up eight dollars this summer; but if I couldn't lay up a cent I should like to be free. I should feel better."

But on the other hand Mrs. Bryce Russell of Lenoir County, North Carolina, gives this amusing account of the opposite reaction:

Grandmother went out to the kitchen to give the news of Lee's surrender to her old cook. She said, "You are free now, Aunt Susan. You are free to leave here and do what you please." After giving that new idea time to register Aunt Susan replied, "Mistis, Marse General Lee ought to be tarred and feathered for doing that!"

There were exceptions to the rule, of course, but Woodrow Wilson who lived in the South through the war and later, presented what was at least the generally prevailing picture of conditions in the following paragraph in his History of the American People:

It was a singular and noteworthy thing, the while, how little the quiet labor of the Negroes was disturbed by the troubles of the time and the absence of their masters. . . . Gentlewomen presided still with unquestioned authority upon the secluded plantations—their husbands, brothers, sons, men and youths alike, gone to the front. Great gangs of cheery Negroes worked in the fields, planted and reaped and garnered and did their lonely mistresses' bidding in all things without restlessness, with quiet industry, with show of faithful affection even.

CHAPTER TEN

Confusion and Chaos at the Confederacy's Capital

ON APRIL 3, 1865, JUST SIX DAYS BEFORE THE SURRENDER AT *Appomattox, the citizens of the Confederacy's capital, not psychologically prepared for any such admission of disaster, were startled to receive the news, "Richmond must be evacuated by midnight!" Immediately thereafter scenes were witnessed which to all who had read Carlyle's* French Revolution *must have seemed strangely reminiscent of the hectic days in Paris at the outbreak of that revolution.*

There was of course in Richmond no such crime and bloodshed as occurred in Paris. But there seems to have been equal chaos and confusion. Power changed from one highly literate class long in undisputed authority to a class almost totally illiterate and wholly unused to power. The Negroes who were one day obedient slaves were suddenly in a position to give orders to their former masters and mistresses. Civilians who had lived in safety through four long years of war suddenly found themselves helpless captives of an occupying enemy army.

Against such a background both the good and bad in human nature assumed exaggerated forms. Many Negroes were insolent but many others remained constant in their affection for former masters and mistresses. Some army officials "clothed in a little brief authority" assumed all the qualities Shakespeare had long before lamented. But others showed courtesy where discourtesy might have been expected.

What really happened in these final days of Richmond as the capital of what had been hoped would become a new nation in a new world? What happened in Paris we may learn from Carlyle who was not there. Very fortunately we may learn what happened in Richmond from a very gifted lady who was there—and wrote the story while it was happening. That lady was Miss Emma Mordecai whose home, Rosewood Plantation, was not far away. In a letter to a friend written from Rosewood April 5, 1865, just 48 hours after Richmond's evacuation, she describes the events as they happened to her, her sister Rose, and her niece Caroline:

Rosewood, April 5th, 1865

My dear Edward,

I must endeavor to command sufficient composure to narrate to you our experience of the last two days, commencing a little before sunset Sunday afternoon, when like the crash of a terrific thunderbolt, the unlooked-for tidings reached us—Richmond was to be evacuated at twelve o'clock that night!

The two days preceding this had been of exquisite beauty and tranquility. I had spent the previous week with friends in Richmond where no apprehensions were entertained of such a calamity. My darling niece Caroline had accompanied me home on Friday to spend a week with me in the country, and it would have been impossible for us to have been less prepared than we were for such an awful, crushing blow.

I need not tell you that language has no power to describe

the dismay, the grief, and the appalling terror produced by such tidings. Lieut. R. J. Moses, who had been lately returned as a paroled prisoner, like a kind friend walked out to let Caroline know, so she might return to town before it was too late, our situation outside the lines seeming more perilous than any in the city. . . . We heard that the enemy were establishing order in the City, had assisted in stopping the fires, and that there was less to apprehend from them than we had supposed. Still we could not but feel fearful, though we went through the usual routine of the morning with outward composure. I again dressed myself with care, and we sat down in the chamber to our knitting—the usual work of Confederate women, but now alas! *we should have no army to work for!* Still the employment made us less nervous.

Massie, a hired Negro boy, went off without asking permission; the first act of insubordination as yet experienced. Cyrus went to work in the field, but we felt no assurance he would continue faithful. The house was closely shut up.

By and by we were startled by the clatter of horse's feet, leaping the fence by the henhouse. Rose was lying down, so I went to the door and saw a Negro dragoon, fully armed, galloping round the house, while another in the woods near by was calling to him in peremptory tones, to "come away directly," which he did, and they rode rapidly away in the direction of Camp Lee. We wondered at our escape, and were rejoiced to find ourselves less terrified than we had expected to be. We resumed our knitting, and endeavoured to resume our composure.

About eleven o'clock we were again startled by the sound of horse's feet in the yard, and again I went to the door. There close by the porch, on a bare-backed horse, sat an insolent looking Negro, dirty and ragged. On seeing me he said, "You got any saddle here? If you have, hand it out." I called to one of the women servants to enquire where Cyrus was, and told her to go up in the field and tell him to come. The Negro said, "If it's the man dat was ploughing, *he* tole me dey was a saddle here—I done got his horse an' now I want de saddle; so han' it out, and be quick 'bout it." I said, "Have you got any paper or order to get these things?" He said, "No, but I got orders to take ev'y horse and saddle outside de lines." The horse he was on was a newly stolen one. I looked around and said, "Is there any officer with you?" "Yes," he said, "yonder de Sergeant," pointing towards the garden; and in the field drawn up close against the garden fence were two Negroes in uniform, mounted and armed.

Meantime, resistance seeming worse than useless with such a ruffian, Rose told Mary to carry out the saddle, and he commenced putting it on in great haste asking if there was no blanket to put under it, to which I replied "NO!" Rose crept out then into the yard and in the direction of the "officer," to try and expostulate with them about taking her only horse, but when they saw her coming, they sent her horse off and rode away before she could get near them.

I felt convinced that these men had no authority for their conduct, and after thinking the matter over, we began to hope it might be possible to get redress. I determined to go myself to Camp Lee—to state the case to the officer in command there, and see what could be done. There was no one to go with me, so we decided that I should take Mary and Georgiana, two little Negro girls, as better than to go entirely alone. I told Rose to pray for me as I set off, and committed my undertaking to God.

Before we reached the outer line of pickets, we saw something moving along the road, looking like a number of persons in a group. On getting nearer we found that a number of *Negro* soldiers in uniform, under the direction of two mounted white officers, were removing a cannon from one of our abandoned batteries to some other point. I hurried on, anxious to get up to them before the officers should ride off. On reaching them I spoke in the most courteous manner to one of the officers, and asked if I should be allowed to pass into the lines. He proved to be a gentleman. I told him my object, and he advised me to go to General Draper's headquarters, and he thought I might get redress. We had some further conversation, and thanking him for his courtesy, I passed on. He soon overtook me, as the cannon he was attending to was moving down the lines, and offered, if it would be agreeable to me, to dismount and let me ride, saying "his animal was a very kind creature." I declined this with thanks, telling him that I should be afraid. He persuaded me to try it, but seeing I objected, did not insist, but rode slowly by my side, talking very pleasantly, and showing me every gentlemanly attention, dismounting to assist me over several streams that ran across the road. When he got to a place where the cannon he was in charge of had to be turned into another road, he gave his men directions and continued with me—past the pickets (black and insolent) into the camp, and up to the headquarters of General Draper, whom I found occupying some of the buildings at Camp Lee. He left me with General Draper, a sleek, dapper, *un*military looking man, who received me very politely, rose and gave me his seat of which there were only two in the room, and after hearing my statement of the conduct of his men, told me it was contrary to orders; that they belonged to the 5th Massachusetts Coloured Cavalry, and if I could see their Colonel (Adams) and identify the horse, it would be restored. . . . So I thanked him and started off with my little escort. The whole place within the Fair grounds, late Camp Lee and now a Yankee Camp, was black and blue with well-equipped Negro troops. Cavalry, Infantry, and Artillery, all enjoying the "dolce far niente" in various ways.

I walked through them majestically (I never in my life had felt so proudly defiant) and met with no rudeness or interruption. The walk from there to the Capitol seemed interminable; and Richmond could no longer be recognized. Yankee officers on fine horses dashing through Broad Street— the sidewalks thronged with people I never saw before, and Negro soldiers, drunk and sober. The population of Sersamersville looked truly joyous and delighted with the new order of things. The blockade was at last raised, and Yankee sutlers were bringing in loads of provisions that had become rarities in the Confederacy. As I advanced down Broad Street toward 6th, the pavement was covered with the plate glass from the fine doors and windows, reduced to powder by the explosions, while rough boards supplied its place. All stores were closed and the street filthy. Close up against Stebbins's handsome china store, on the sidewalk, was backed up an immense Yankee Ordnance wagon—without horses. . . . I had to pass through what might well be called a *nasty* crowd, but I met with no rudeness, and was, myself, studiously polite and dignified.

Our remaining information from Miss Mordecai comes from a diary she kept beginning ten days later, April 16, 1865:

April 16—Mr. Sinton called to leave the money, $1.50 in little Yankee notes, he got for the salad yesterday. He told us it was certain General Lee had surrendered—that he had seen several of the disbanded soldiers returning to their homes, and they told him of the safety of our boys—I don't know why but we doubt the truth of this last piece of information. General Lee arrived in Richmond yesterday he says. . . . Soon after he left us, we heard the footsteps of men approaching the house—of course we expected Yankees— It was John and George [Miss Mordecai's nephews] safe and well! Willie got separated from them but was on his way with a mule he had been allowed to bring out with him. So they are all unhurt after such dangers, and exposure—privation and fatigue and hardships, as God's mercy and protection alone could have preserved them through. For five days and nights, they had marched and fought continuously, without one hour's sleep. They speak in grateful terms of the enemy's conduct to them after the surrender. General Lee came along with them accompanied by his staff, his wagons, ambulance etc. General Grant refused to take his sword.

Rose was overcome at seeing the boys. She had despaired of ever seeing them all three again, and here they are—not a hair of their heads injured. What a wonderful mercy! They had walked thirty miles yesterday. They are wonderfully cheerful, but like General Lee they have the comfort of knowing they have done their whole duty as brave constant soldiers.

May 6—The servants *all* went Friday evening—Georgiana and Martha returned at dusk and are still with us. They behave well so far, and are very useful. . . . Poor Rose is miserably depressed. She scarcely slept at all Friday night. She is not only entirely upset in her domestic affairs, but she is grieved to part with Cy and Sarah and Lizzy. She said, "If they felt as *I* do, they could not possibly leave me." Cy came back yesterday after his fowls, and sought an opportunity to take leave of his "Mistiss" (as he still calls Rose in spite of his declaration to me to the contrary) and of the boys. He expressed to Rose his regret for his improper conduct the other morning, and was very much affected at parting with her. She could not take leave of him without emotion, and has felt miserable ever since. What an uprooting of social ties, and tearing asunder of almost kindred associations and destruction of true loyalty, this strange, new state of things produced! ! The disturbance to the whites and the privations it will at first entail upon the poor, improvident Negroes is incalculable.

CHAPTER ELEVEN

A Prodigal Soldier's Return

No PICTURE OF THE CIVIL WAR COULD BE COMPLETE UNLESS IT *included the father and mother of the son in uniform—often waiting, waiting for a too-long-delayed return. Sometimes the soldier had never learned to write and so depended on some oral message, possibly lost in transmission. At any rate not a few soldiers far from home returned months after—and in some cases a year or so after the war—with no advance word to wife or parents. With charm and authenticity Dr. J. Frank Dobie of the University of Texas here reveals what war meant to one such waiting couple in pioneer Texas cattle country—a true story sent for special inclusion in this volume.*

Not long after Texas joined the Confederacy, a youngster named Tim Cude, from Live Oak County, enlisted. Although he was only sixteen years old, his way with oxen was a community wonder—especially the power of his voice over them. It was a voice young and lush, but strong, without the gosling quality. He did not charm the oxen by whispering—horse-charmer style—in their ears.

Brindle and Whitey were his wheelers, Sam Houston and Davy Crockett, the leaders. They were steers of the old-time Texas Longhorn breed, and they could pull a log out of its bark. When Tim commanded them they would go to their places to be hitched to wagon or plow. Tim was partial to Brindle, and when he put a hand over the ox's head, the ox would often show his pleasure by licking out his tongue. The four oxen were the last inhabitants of the little Cude ranch that Tim told good-by when he left to fight the Yankees. He was an only child. He did not realize what emptiness he left behind him. He seldom wrote to relieve it.

Months after Appomattox, his mother and father learned that he had been alive at Lee's surrender. More months, then a year, then two years, dragged by, and still Tim did not come home, and there was no word from him. At first his father and mother talked with high hopes of his coming. Then, gradually, they came to say little, even to each other, about his return. They still nursed a hope, but the heavy conviction settled down on them that Tim must be among the many boys in gray who would never come back home. Their hope grew gray and secret, without confidence. The days went by as slow as laboring oxen walk.

In the late spring of 1867, Mr. Cude put a few beeves in a herd going north. Six months later the owners of the herd returned and paid him the first money he had seen in years. The aging couple needed to buy necessities, but Mr. Cude had a hard time persuading "mama" to go with him down to Powderhorn on the coast for the purchases. "Tim might come while we are gone," was her only argument. Mr. Cude's argument that, if he came, he would stay until they got back, had slight weight with her. She wanted to be there. Mr. Cude would not argue, not even to himself, much less to her, that Tim would never come. But he often reasoned gently that it was better for them both to be resigned.

It was in December before Mrs. Cude finally consented to go. They took a load of dry cowhides with them, and as the oxen pulled them south at the rate of about two miles an hour, they went over their plans again and again for spending the money.

The plans cheered them. They would buy sacks of real coffee and a new coffee grinder that would do away with the labor of pounding the grains held by canvas with a hammer. They would buy sacks of flour and have real flour bread. "You remember how Tim always likes flour gravy," Mrs. Cude said, "and sugar—sugar for cakes and pies." She would have enough calico for three new dresses and a sunbonnet, besides a tablecloth; he would have new boots, new hat and breeches, and percale for sewing into shirts. "I'll get some blue for Tim," Mrs. Cude said. There would be a new plow for the cornpatch and lumber for a gallery to the frame house, so hot in the summer. They needed chains, axes, many ordinary things.

It took them a week to get down to Powderhorn, and then two days to buy everything and load the wagon. On the way back Mrs. Cude kept wishing they'd make better time, but the four old tortoise-stepping oxen never moved a foot faster. "Perhaps Tim came home today," Mrs. Cude would say at the evening camp. "I dreamed last night that he came just after dark," she'd say over the morning campfire, always burning long before daybreak. In all the dragging months, months adding themselves into years, no day had dawned, no night had fallen, that she had not made some little extra preparation for her boy's coming home. In all the period of waiting, this was the first time she had not been there to welcome him. As she approached the waiting homestead now, the hopes of more than fourteen absent days and of more than fourteen absent nights were all accumulated into one hope. Perhaps Tim had come! Mr. Cude shared the hope, too, but it hurt him to see "mama" disappointed, and he never encouraged daydreams.

At last they were only six miles from home. Christmas

was only three days away. Then in a mudhole at the crossing on La Parra Creek the oxen stalled. For an hour Mr. Cude struggled and worried with them, trying to get them to make the supreme pull. Mrs. Cude threw all her strength on the spoke of one wheel. Finally Mr. Cude began the weary business of unloading some of the freight and carrying it on his back up the bank from the creek.

Then suddenly they were aware of a man, dismounted from the horse beside him, standing on the bank just ahead. Being down in the creek, they could not have seen his approach. His frame, though lank, was well filled out, his face all bearded, his clothes nondescript. In his posture was something of the soldier. Nearly all Southern men had, in those days, been soldiers. For a second he seemed to be holding something back; then he gave a hearty greeting that was cordially responded to.

"Those look like mighty good oxen," the young man said, coming down, as any stranger in that country at that time would come to help anybody in a tight spot.

"They are good oxen, but they won't pull this wagon out now," Mr. Cude answered. "I guess they're getting old like us and can't. We've been working them since before the war."

The stranger had moved around so that he was very near the wheel oxen, which he faced, instead of the driver and his wife. His hand was on Brindle's head, between the long rough horns, and the old ox, whose countenance was the same whether in a bog hole or a patch of spring tallow weed, licked out his tongue.

"I believe I can make these old boys haul the wagon out," the man said.

"They wouldn't do any better for a stranger than for their master," Mr. Cude answered.

"There's only one person who could get them to pull,"

added Mrs. Cude. "That's our boy who went to the war."

"Did he know oxen?" the young man asked out of his beard.

"Oh, yes, and they knew him. They liked him."

Then for a little while there was silence.

As Mr. Cude began drawing up his rawhide whip, again the stranger asked for a chance to try his hand.

"Very well," Mr. Cude agreed slowly, "but every time you try to make 'em pull and they don't budge the wagon, they're that much harder to get against the yoke the next time."

The young man asked the names of the oxen and got them. Then he took the long whip, not to lash the animals—for that was not the whip's function—but to pop it. He swung it lightly and tested the popper three or four times, as if getting back the feel of something long familiar that had been laid aside. Then he curved the fifteen feet of tapering plaited rawhide through the air—and the ringing crack made the sky brighter. At the same time he began calling to the oxen to come on and pull. He talked to Brindle and Whitey and Sam Houston and Davy Crockett harder than a crapshooter talking to his bones.

The oxen, without a jerk, lay slowly, steadily, mightily, into the yokes. The wheels began to turn. The whip popped again, like a crack of lightning in the sky, and the strong voice rose, pleading, encouraging, confident, dominating.

The oxen were halfway up the bank now. They pulled on out, but nobody was talking to them any longer. For with a shout that rang to the Texas heavens the Cudes recognized their son who could handle oxen as no one else on earth. And no welcome of feast and fatted calf ever overwhelmed a prodigal son like that, initiated by four faithful old oxen, which Tim Cude received from his mother and father on the banks of an insignificant creek in a wilderness of mesquite and prairie.

The Enduring Glory of Their Courage

As this review of four years of fighting comes to an end, nothing could be more fitting than to pay a word of tribute to an army whose members then proved themselves as superb in defeat as they had been in victory. Certainly in no triumph over the enemy was the character of their warrior-chieftain Robert E. Lee more resplendent than when, returning to the Union he had so reluctantly left, he appealed to all Southerners for genuine peace and reconciliation—for "the allayment of passion, the dissipation of prejudice, and the restoration of reason." And able General Robert F. Hoke, reduced by Appomattox to the necessity of following a plow over his farmlands, could say with equal truth and dignity, "I like this better than shooting Yankees."

It seems a fair appraisal of both armies that was made not long after Appomattox by John Esten Cooke, one of the most noted Confederate authors: "Both armies had shown a gallantry that extorted the admiration of their adversaries. They were not a foe to be despised, nor did either side despise the other in that hard struggle. When General Lee surrendered, it was [a few] non-combatants, not the Northern troops, who wanted every Southern soldier hanged or shot for treason."

Nor should any Southerner wish for any higher authority

than Winston Churchill for the statement that the courage of the Southern people which caused them to fight on for two years after their cause was hopeless is "one of the enduring glories of the American people." Nor can I ever forget that it was a former Confederate general, Stephen D. Lee, then president of Mississippi Agricultural and Mechanical College, who once said to me, "Great as was the courage shown by the Southern people in four years of war they showed even greater courage in the eleven long years of Reconstruction."

Furthermore, in both war and peace the courage of Southern women fully equaled the courage of Southern men. Soldiers defeated in battle but unbowed by defeat worked on in their untiring efforts to rebuild a wasted land with a determination expressed by the indomitable Scarlett O'Hara's "Tomorrow is another day!" So my own grandmother when my grandfather Poe sadly reported the irretrievable freeing of the slaves, answered courageously, "Give me back my boys and we will let the darkeys go!"

Perhaps therefore we cannot more fittingly conclude this volume than by noting that after all the losses and sorrows Mrs. Edmondston had suffered—as reported in the diary from which we have quoted so extensively—she ended that diary with this simple but significant entry:

"December 31—So ends this terrible year of 1865. Thank God it is over! So now to our eggnog and brighter hopes for 1866."

Index

A CATALOG OF SELECTED
DOVER BOOKS
IN ALL FIELDS OF INTEREST

A CATALOG OF SELECTED DOVER
BOOKS IN ALL FIELDS OF INTEREST

CONCERNING THE SPIRITUAL IN ART, Wassily Kandinsky. Pioneering work by father of abstract art. Thoughts on color theory, nature of art. Analysis of earlier masters. 12 illustrations. 80pp. of text. 5⅜ x 8½. 23411-8 Pa. $3.95

ANIMALS: 1,419 Copyright-Free Illustrations of Mammals, Birds, Fish, Insects, etc., Jim Harter (ed.). Clear wood engravings present, in extremely lifelike poses, over 1,000 species of animals. One of the most extensive pictorial sourcebooks of its kind. Captions. Index. 284pp. 9 x 12. 23766-4 Pa. $12.95

CELTIC ART: The Methods of Construction, George Bain. Simple geometric techniques for making Celtic interlacements, spirals, Kells-type initials, animals, humans, etc. Over 500 illustrations. 160pp. 9 x 12. (USO) 22923-8 Pa. $9.95

AN ATLAS OF ANATOMY FOR ARTISTS, Fritz Schider. Most thorough reference work on art anatomy in the world. Hundreds of illustrations, including selections from works by Vesalius, Leonardo, Goya, Ingres, Michelangelo, others. 593 illustrations. 192pp. 7⅛ x 10¼. 20241-0 Pa. $9 95

CELTIC HAND STROKE-BY-STROKE (Irish Half-Uncial from "The Book of Kells"): An Arthur Baker Calligraphy Manual, Arthur Baker. Complete guide to creating each letter of the alphabet in distinctive Celtic manner. Covers hand position, strokes, pens, inks, paper, more. Illustrated. 48pp. 8¼ x 11. 24336-2 Pa. $3.95

EASY ORIGAMI, John Montroll. Charming collection of 32 projects (hat, cup, pelican, piano, swan, many more) specially designed for the novice origami hobbyist. Clearly illustrated easy-to-follow instructions insure that even beginning papercrafters will achieve successful results. 48pp. 8¼ x 11. 27298-2 Pa. $2.95

THE COMPLETE BOOK OF BIRDHOUSE CONSTRUCTION FOR WOOD-WORKERS, Scott D. Campbell. Detailed instructions, illustrations, tables. Also data on bird habitat and instinct patterns. Bibliography. 3 tables. 63 illustrations in 15 figures. 48pp. 5¼ x 8½. 24407-5 Pa. $2.50

BLOOMINGDALE'S ILLUSTRATED 1886 CATALOG: Fashions, Dry Goods and Housewares, Bloomingdale Brothers. Famed merchants' extremely rare catalog depicting about 1,700 products: clothing, housewares, firearms, dry goods, jewelry, more. Invaluable for dating, identifying vintage items. Also, copyright-free graphics for artists, designers. Co-published with Henry Ford Museum & Greenfield Village. 160pp. 8¼ x 11. 25780-0 Pa. $9.95

HISTORIC COSTUME IN PICTURES, Braun & Schneider. Over 1,450 costumed figures in clearly detailed engravings–from dawn of civilization to end of 19th century. Captions. Many folk costumes. 256pp. 8⅜ x 11¾. 23150-X Pa. $12.95

STICKLEY CRAFTSMAN FURNITURE CATALOGS, Gustav Stickley and L. & J. G. Stickley. Beautiful, functional furniture in two authentic catalogs from 1910. 594 illustrations, including 277 photos, show settles, rockers, armchairs, reclining chairs, bookcases, desks, tables. 183pp. 6½ x 9¼. 23838-5 Pa. $9.95

AMERICAN LOCOMOTIVES IN HISTORIC PHOTOGRAPHS: 1858 to 1949, Ron Ziel (ed.). A rare collection of 126 meticulously detailed official photographs, called "builder portraits," of American locomotives that majestically chronicle the rise of steam locomotive power in America. Introduction. Detailed captions. xi + 129pp. 9 x 12. 27393-8 Pa. $12.95

AMERICA'S LIGHTHOUSES: An Illustrated History, Francis Ross Holland, Jr. Delightfully written, profusely illustrated fact-filled survey of over 200 American lighthouses since 1716. History, anecdotes, technological advances, more. 240pp. 8 x 10¾. 25576-X Pa. $12.95

TOWARDS A NEW ARCHITECTURE, Le Corbusier. Pioneering manifesto by founder of "International School." Technical and aesthetic theories, views of industry, economics, relation of form to function, "mass-production split" and much more. Profusely illustrated. 320pp. 6⅛ x 9¼. (USO) 25023-7 Pa. $9.95

HOW THE OTHER HALF LIVES, Jacob Riis. Famous journalistic record, exposing poverty and degradation of New York slums around 1900, by major social reformer. 100 striking and influential photographs. 233pp. 10 x 7⅞. 22012-5 Pa. $10.95

FRUIT KEY AND TWIG KEY TO TREES AND SHRUBS, William M. Harlow. One of the handiest and most widely used identification aids. Fruit key covers 120 deciduous and evergreen species; twig key 160 deciduous species. Easily used. Over 300 photographs. 126pp. 5⅜ x 8½. 20511-8 Pa. $3.95

COMMON BIRD SONGS, Dr. Donald J. Borror. Songs of 60 most common U.S. birds: robins, sparrows, cardinals, bluejays, finches, more—arranged in order of increasing complexity. Up to 9 variations of songs of each species.
Cassette and manual 99911-4 $8.95

ORCHIDS AS HOUSE PLANTS, Rebecca Tyson Northen. Grow cattleyas and many other kinds of orchids—in a window, in a case, or under artificial light. 63 illustrations. 148pp. 5⅜ x 8½. 23261-1 Pa. $4.95

MONSTER MAZES, Dave Phillips. Masterful mazes at four levels of difficulty. Avoid deadly perils and evil creatures to find magical treasures. Solutions for all 32 exciting illustrated puzzles. 48pp. 8¼ x 11. 26005-4 Pa. $2.95

MOZART'S DON GIOVANNI (DOVER OPERA LIBRETTO SERIES), Wolfgang Amadeus Mozart. Introduced and translated by Ellen H. Bleiler. Standard Italian libretto, with complete English translation. Convenient and thoroughly portable—an ideal companion for reading along with a recording or the performance itself. Introduction. List of characters. Plot summary. 121pp. 5¼ x 8½. 24944-1 Pa. $2.95

TECHNICAL MANUAL AND DICTIONARY OF CLASSICAL BALLET, Gail Grant. Defines, explains, comments on steps, movements, poses and concepts. 15-page pictorial section. Basic book for student, viewer. 127pp. 5⅜ x 8½. 21843-0 Pa. $4.95

BRASS INSTRUMENTS: Their History and Development, Anthony Baines. Authoritative, updated survey of the evolution of trumpets, trombones, bugles, cornets, French horns, tubas and other brass wind instruments. Over 140 illustrations and 48 music examples. Corrected and updated by author. New preface. Bibliography. 320pp. 5⅜ x 8½. 27574-4 Pa. $9.95

HOLLYWOOD GLAMOR PORTRAITS, John Kobal (ed.). 145 photos from 1926-49. Harlow, Gable, Bogart, Bacall; 94 stars in all. Full background on photographers, technical aspects. 160pp. 8⅜ x 11¼. 23352-9 Pa. $11.95

MAX AND MORITZ, Wilhelm Busch. Great humor classic in both German and English. Also 10 other works: "Cat and Mouse," "Plisch and Plumm," etc. 216pp. 5⅜ x 8½. 20181-3 Pa. $6.95

THE RAVEN AND OTHER FAVORITE POEMS, Edgar Allan Poe. Over 40 of the author's most memorable poems: "The Bells," "Ulalume," "Israfel," "To Helen," "The Conqueror Worm," "Eldorado," "Annabel Lee," many more. Alphabetic lists of titles and first lines. 64pp. 5³⁄₁₆ x 8¼. 26685-0 Pa. $1.00

PERSONAL MEMOIRS OF U. S. GRANT, Ulysses Simpson Grant. Intelligent, deeply moving firsthand account of Civil War campaigns, considered by many the finest military memoirs ever written. Includes letters, historic photographs, maps and more. 528pp. 6⅛ x 9¼. 28587-1 Pa. $11.95

AMULETS AND SUPERSTITIONS, E. A. Wallis Budge. Comprehensive discourse on origin, powers of amulets in many ancient cultures: Arab, Persian Babylonian, Assyrian, Egyptian, Gnostic, Hebrew, Phoenician, Syriac, etc. Covers cross, swastika, crucifix, seals, rings, stones, etc. 584pp. 5⅜ x 8½. 23573-4 Pa. $12.95

RUSSIAN STORIES/PYCCKNE PACCKA3bl: A Dual-Language Book, edited by Gleb Struve. Twelve tales by such masters as Chekhov, Tolstoy, Dostoevsky, Pushkin, others. Excellent word-for-word English translations on facing pages, plus teaching and study aids, Russian/English vocabulary, biographical/critical introductions, more. 416pp. 5⅜ x 8½. 26244-8 Pa. $8.95

PHILADELPHIA THEN AND NOW: 60 Sites Photographed in the Past and Present, Kenneth Finkel and Susan Oyama. Rare photographs of City Hall, Logan Square, Independence Hall, Betsy Ross House, other landmarks juxtaposed with contemporary views. Captures changing face of historic city. Introduction. Captions. 128pp. 8¼ x 11. 25790-8 Pa. $9.95

AIA ARCHITECTURAL GUIDE TO NASSAU AND SUFFOLK COUNTIES, LONG ISLAND, The American Institute of Architects, Long Island Chapter, and the Society for the Preservation of Long Island Antiquities. Comprehensive, well-researched and generously illustrated volume brings to life over three centuries of Long Island's great architectural heritage. More than 240 photographs with authoritative, extensively detailed captions. 176pp. 8¼ x 11. 26946-9 Pa. $14.95

NORTH AMERICAN INDIAN LIFE: Customs and Traditions of 23 Tribes, Elsie Clews Parsons (ed.). 27 fictionalized essays by noted anthropologists examine religion, customs, government, additional facets of life among the Winnebago, Crow, Zuni, Eskimo, other tribes. 480pp. 6⅛ x 9¼. 27377-6 Pa. $10.95

FRANK LLOYD WRIGHT'S HOLLYHOCK HOUSE, Donald Hoffmann. Lavishly illustrated, carefully documented study of one of Wright's most controversial residential designs. Over 120 photographs, floor plans, elevations, etc. Detailed perceptive text by noted Wright scholar. Index. 128pp. 9¼ x 10¾. 27133-1 Pa. $11.95

THE MALE AND FEMALE FIGURE IN MOTION: 60 Classic Photographic Sequences, Eadweard Muybridge. 60 true-action photographs of men and women walking, running, climbing, bending, turning, etc., reproduced from rare 19th-century masterpiece. vi + 121pp. 9 x 12. 24745-7 Pa. $10.95

1001 QUESTIONS ANSWERED ABOUT THE SEASHORE, N. J. Berrill and Jacquelyn Berrill. Queries answered about dolphins, sea snails, sponges, starfish, fishes, shore birds, many others. Covers appearance, breeding, growth, feeding, much more. 305pp. 5¼ x 8¼. 23366-9 Pa. $8.95

GUIDE TO OWL WATCHING IN NORTH AMERICA, Donald S. Heintzelman. Superb guide offers complete data and descriptions of 19 species: barn owl, screech owl, snowy owl, many more. Expert coverage of owl-watching equipment, conservation, migrations and invasions, etc. Guide to observing sites. 84 illustrations. xiii + 193pp. 5⅜ x 8½. 27344-X Pa. $8.95

MEDICINAL AND OTHER USES OF NORTH AMERICAN PLANTS: A Historical Survey with Special Reference to the Eastern Indian Tribes, Charlotte Erichsen-Brown. Chronological historical citations document 500 years of usage of plants, trees, shrubs native to eastern Canada, northeastern U.S. Also complete identifying information. 343 illustrations. 544pp. 6½ x 9¼. 25951-X Pa. $12.95

STORYBOOK MAZES, Dave Phillips. 23 stories and mazes on two-page spreads: Wizard of Oz, Treasure Island, Robin Hood, etc. Solutions. 64pp. 8¼ x 11. 23628-5 Pa. $2.95

NEGRO FOLK MUSIC, U.S.A., Harold Courlander. Noted folklorist's scholarly yet readable analysis of rich and varied musical tradition. Includes authentic versions of over 40 folk songs. Valuable bibliography and discography. xi + 324pp. 5⅜ x 8½. 27350-4 Pa. $7.95

MOVIE-STAR PORTRAITS OF THE FORTIES, John Kobal (ed.). 163 glamor, studio photos of 106 stars of the 1940s: Rita Hayworth, Ava Gardner, Marlon Brando, Clark Gable, many more. 176pp. 8⅜ x 11¼. 23546-7 Pa. $12.95

BENCHLEY LOST AND FOUND, Robert Benchley. Finest humor from early 30s, about pet peeves, child psychologists, post office and others. Mostly unavailable elsewhere. 73 illustrations by Peter Arno and others. 183pp. 5⅜ x 8½. 22410-4 Pa. $6.95

YEKL and THE IMPORTED BRIDEGROOM AND OTHER STORIES OF YIDDISH NEW YORK, Abraham Cahan. Film Hester Street based on Yekl (1896). Novel, other stories among first about Jewish immigrants on N.Y.'s East Side. 240pp. 5⅜ x 8½. 22427-9 Pa. $6.95

SELECTED POEMS, Walt Whitman. Generous sampling from *Leaves of Grass*. Twenty-four poems include "I Hear America Singing," "Song of the Open Road," "I Sing the Body Electric," "When Lilacs Last in the Dooryard Bloom'd," "O Captain! My Captain!"–all reprinted from an authoritative edition. Lists of titles and first lines. 128pp. $5\frac{3}{16}$ x 8¼. 26878-0 Pa. $1.00

CATALOG OF DOVER BOOKS

THE BEST TALES OF HOFFMANN, E. T. A. Hoffmann. 10 of Hoffmann's most important stories: "Nutcracker and the King of Mice," "The Golden Flowerpot," etc. 458pp. 5⅜ x 8½. 21793-0 Pa. $9.95

FROM FETISH TO GOD IN ANCIENT EGYPT, E. A. Wallis Budge. Rich detailed survey of Egyptian conception of "God" and gods, magic, cult of animals, Osiris, more. Also, superb English translations of hymns and legends. 240 illustrations. 545pp. 5⅜ x 8½. 25803-3 Pa. $11.95

FRENCH STORIES/CONTES FRANÇAIS: A Dual-Language Book, Wallace Fowlie. Ten stories by French masters, Voltaire to Camus: "Micromegas" by Voltaire; "The Atheist's Mass" by Balzac; "Minuet" by de Maupassant; "The Guest" by Camus, six more. Excellent English translations on facing pages. Also French-English vocabulary list, exercises, more. 352pp. 5⅜ x 8½. 26443-2 Pa. $8.95

CHICAGO AT THE TURN OF THE CENTURY IN PHOTOGRAPHS: 122 Historic Views from the Collections of the Chicago Historical Society, Larry A. Viskochil. Rare large-format prints offer detailed views of City Hall, State Street, the Loop, Hull House, Union Station, many other landmarks, circa 1904-1913. Introduction. Captions. Maps. 144pp. 9⅜ x 12¼. 24656-6 Pa. $12.95

OLD BROOKLYN IN EARLY PHOTOGRAPHS, 1865-1929, William Lee Younger. Luna Park, Gravesend race track, construction of Grand Army Plaza, moving of Hotel Brighton, etc. 157 previously unpublished photographs. 165pp. 8⅞ x 11¾. 23587-4 Pa. $13.95

THE MYTHS OF THE NORTH AMERICAN INDIANS, Lewis Spence. Rich anthology of the myths and legends of the Algonquins, Iroquois, Pawnees and Sioux, prefaced by an extensive historical and ethnological commentary. 36 illustrations. 480pp. 5⅜ x 8½. 25967-6 Pa. $8.95

AN ENCYCLOPEDIA OF BATTLES: Accounts of Over 1,560 Battles from 1479 B.C. to the Present, David Eggenberger. Essential details of every major battle in recorded history from the first battle of Megiddo in 1479 B.C. to Grenada in 1984. List of Battle Maps. New Appendix covering the years 1967-1984. Index. 99 illustrations. 544pp. 6½ x 9¼. 24913-1 Pa. $14.95

SAILING ALONE AROUND THE WORLD, Captain Joshua Slocum. First man to sail around the world, alone, in small boat. One of great feats of seamanship told in delightful manner. 67 illustrations. 294pp. 5⅜ x 8½. 20326-3 Pa. $5.95

ANARCHISM AND OTHER ESSAYS, Emma Goldman. Powerful, penetrating, prophetic essays on direct action, role of minorities, prison reform, puritan hypocrisy, violence, etc. 271pp. 5⅜ x 8½. 22484-8 Pa. $6.95

MYTHS OF THE HINDUS AND BUDDHISTS, Ananda K. Coomaraswamy and Sister Nivedita. Great stories of the epics; deeds of Krishna, Shiva, taken from puranas, Vedas, folk tales; etc. 32 illustrations. 400pp. 5⅜ x 8½. 21759-0 Pa. $10.95

BEYOND PSYCHOLOGY, Otto Rank. Fear of death, desire of immortality, nature of sexuality, social organization, creativity, according to Rankian system. 291pp. 5⅜ x 8½. 20485-5 Pa. $8.95

A THEOLOGICO-POLITICAL TREATISE, Benedict Spinoza. Also contains unfinished Political Treatise. Great classic on religious liberty, theory of government on common consent. R. Elwes translation. Total of 421pp. 5⅜ x 8½. 20249-6 Pa. $9.95

MY BONDAGE AND MY FREEDOM, Frederick Douglass. Born a slave, Douglass became outspoken force in antislavery movement. The best of Douglass' autobiographies. Graphic description of slave life. 464pp. 5⅜ x 8½. 22457-0 Pa. $8.95

FOLLOWING THE EQUATOR: A Journey Around the World, Mark Twain. Fascinating humorous account of 1897 voyage to Hawaii, Australia, India, New Zealand, etc. Ironic, bemused reports on peoples, customs, climate, flora and fauna, politics, much more. 197 illustrations. 720pp. 5⅜ x 8½. 26113-1 Pa. $15.95

THE PEOPLE CALLED SHAKERS, Edward D. Andrews. Definitive study of Shakers: origins, beliefs, practices, dances, social organization, furniture and crafts, etc. 33 illustrations. 351pp. 5⅜ x 8½. 21081-2 Pa. $8.95

THE MYTHS OF GREECE AND ROME, H. A. Guerber. A classic of mythology, generously illustrated, long prized for its simple, graphic, accurate retelling of the principal myths of Greece and Rome, and for its commentary on their origins and significance. With 64 illustrations by Michelangelo, Raphael, Titian, Rubens, Canova, Bernini and others. 480pp. 5⅜ x 8½. 27584-1 Pa. $9.95

PSYCHOLOGY OF MUSIC, Carl E. Seashore. Classic work discusses music as a medium from psychological viewpoint. Clear treatment of physical acoustics, auditory apparatus, sound perception, development of musical skills, nature of musical feeling, host of other topics. 88 figures. 408pp. 5⅜ x 8½. 21851-1 Pa. $10.95

THE PHILOSOPHY OF HISTORY, Georg W. Hegel. Great classic of Western thought develops concept that history is not chance but rational process, the evolution of freedom. 457pp. 5⅜ x 8½. 20112-0 Pa. $9.95

THE BOOK OF TEA, Kakuzo Okakura. Minor classic of the Orient: entertaining, charming explanation, interpretation of traditional Japanese culture in terms of tea ceremony. 94pp. 5⅜ x 8½. 20070-1 Pa. $3.95

LIFE IN ANCIENT EGYPT, Adolf Erman. Fullest, most thorough, detailed older account with much not in more recent books, domestic life, religion, magic, medicine, commerce, much more. Many illustrations reproduce tomb paintings, carvings, hieroglyphs, etc. 597pp. 5⅜ x 8½. 22632-8 Pa. $11.95

SUNDIALS, Their Theory and Construction, Albert Waugh. Far and away the best, most thorough coverage of ideas, mathematics concerned, types, construction, adjusting anywhere. Simple, nontechnical treatment allows even children to build several of these dials. Over 100 illustrations. 230pp. 5⅜ x 8½. 22947-5 Pa. $7.95

DYNAMICS OF FLUIDS IN POROUS MEDIA, Jacob Bear. For advanced students of ground water hydrology, soil mechanics and physics, drainage and irrigation engineering, and more. 335 illustrations. Exercises, with answers. 784pp. 6⅛ x 9¼. 65675-6 Pa. $19.95

SONGS OF EXPERIENCE: Facsimile Reproduction with 26 Plates in Full Color, William Blake. 26 full-color plates from a rare 1826 edition. Includes "TheTyger," "London," "Holy Thursday," and other poems. Printed text of poems. 48pp. 5¼ x 7. 24636-1 Pa. $4.95

OLD-TIME VIGNETTES IN FULL COLOR, Carol Belanger Grafton (ed.). Over 390 charming, often sentimental illustrations, selected from archives of Victorian graphics—pretty women posing, children playing, food, flowers, kittens and puppies, smiling cherubs, birds and butterflies, much more. All copyright-free. 48pp. 9¼ x 12¼. 27269-9 Pa. $5.95

PERSPECTIVE FOR ARTISTS, Rex Vicat Cole. Depth, perspective of sky and sea, shadows, much more, not usually covered. 391 diagrams, 81 reproductions of drawings and paintings. 279pp. 5⅜ x 8½. 22487-2 Pa. $6.95

DRAWING THE LIVING FIGURE, Joseph Sheppard. Innovative approach to artistic anatomy focuses on specifics of surface anatomy, rather than muscles and bones. Over 170 drawings of live models in front, back and side views, and in widely varying poses. Accompanying diagrams. 177 illustrations. Introduction. Index. 144pp. 8⅜ x11¼. 26723-7 Pa. $8.95

GOTHIC AND OLD ENGLISH ALPHABETS: 100 Complete Fonts, Dan X. Solo. Add power, elegance to posters, signs, other graphics with 100 stunning copyright-free alphabets: Blackstone, Dolbey, Germania, 97 more–including many lower-case, numerals, punctuation marks. 104pp. 8⅛ x 11. 24695-7 Pa. $8.95

HOW TO DO BEADWORK, Mary White. Fundamental book on craft from simple projects to five-bead chains and woven works. 106 illustrations. 142pp. 5⅜ x 8. 20697-1 Pa. $4.95

THE BOOK OF WOOD CARVING, Charles Marshall Sayers. Finest book for beginners discusses fundamentals and offers 34 designs. "Absolutely first rate . . . well thought out and well executed."–E. J. Tangerman. 118pp. 7¾ x 10⅝. 23654-4 Pa. $6.95

ILLUSTRATED CATALOG OF CIVIL WAR MILITARY GOODS: Union Army Weapons, Insignia, Uniform Accessories, and Other Equipment, Schuyler, Hartley, and Graham. Rare, profusely illustrated 1846 catalog includes Union Army uniform and dress regulations, arms and ammunition, coats, insignia, flags, swords, rifles, etc. 226 illustrations. 160pp. 9 x 12. 24939-5 Pa. $10.95

WOMEN'S FASHIONS OF THE EARLY 1900s: An Unabridged Republication of "New York Fashions, 1909," National Cloak & Suit Co. Rare catalog of mail-order fashions documents women's and children's clothing styles shortly after the turn of the century. Captions offer full descriptions, prices. Invaluable resource for fashion, costume historians. Approximately 725 illustrations. 128pp. 8⅜ x 11¼. 27276-1 Pa. $11.95

THE 1912 AND 1915 GUSTAV STICKLEY FURNITURE CATALOGS, Gustav Stickley. With over 200 detailed illustrations and descriptions, these two catalogs are essential reading and reference materials and identification guides for Stickley furniture. Captions cite materials, dimensions and prices. 112pp. 6½ x 9¼. 26676-1 Pa. $9.95

EARLY AMERICAN LOCOMOTIVES, John H. White, Jr. Finest locomotive engravings from early 19th century: historical (1804–74), main-line (after 1870), special, foreign, etc. 147 plates. 142pp. 11⅜ x 8¼. 22772-3 Pa. $10.95

THE TALL SHIPS OF TODAY IN PHOTOGRAPHS, Frank O. Braynard. Lavishly illustrated tribute to nearly 100 majestic contemporary sailing vessels: Amerigo Vespucci, Clearwater, Constitution, Eagle, Mayflower, Sea Cloud, Victory, many more. Authoritative captions provide statistics, background on each ship. 190 black-and-white photographs and illustrations. Introduction. 128pp. 8⅞ x 11¾. 27163-3 Pa. $13.95

EARLY NINETEENTH-CENTURY CRAFTS AND TRADES, Peter Stockham (ed.). Extremely rare 1807 volume describes to youngsters the crafts and trades of the day: brickmaker, weaver, dressmaker, bookbinder, ropemaker, saddler, many more. Quaint prose, charming illustrations for each craft. 20 black-and-white line illustrations. 192pp. 4⅝ x 6.   27293-1 Pa. $4.95

VICTORIAN FASHIONS AND COSTUMES FROM HARPER'S BAZAR, 1867–1898, Stella Blum (ed.). Day costumes, evening wear, sports clothes, shoes, hats, other accessories in over 1,000 detailed engravings. 320pp. 9⅜ x 12¼.
22990-4 Pa. $14.95

GUSTAV STICKLEY, THE CRAFTSMAN, Mary Ann Smith. Superb study surveys broad scope of Stickley's achievement, especially in architecture. Design philosophy, rise and fall of the Craftsman empire, descriptions and floor plans for many Craftsman houses, more. 86 black-and-white halftones. 31 line illustrations. Introduction 208pp. 6½ x 9¼.   27210-9 Pa. $9.95

THE LONG ISLAND RAIL ROAD IN EARLY PHOTOGRAPHS, Ron Ziel. Over 220 rare photos, informative text document origin (1844) and development of rail service on Long Island. Vintage views of early trains, locomotives, stations, passengers, crews, much more. Captions. 8⅞ x 11¾.   26301-0 Pa. $13.95

THE BOOK OF OLD SHIPS: From Egyptian Galleys to Clipper Ships, Henry B. Culver. Superb, authoritative history of sailing vessels, with 80 magnificent line illustrations. Galley, bark, caravel, longship, whaler, many more. Detailed, informative text on each vessel by noted naval historian. Introduction. 256pp. 5⅜ x 8½.
27332-6 Pa. $7.95

TEN BOOKS ON ARCHITECTURE, Vitruvius. The most important book ever written on architecture. Early Roman aesthetics, technology, classical orders, site selection, all other aspects. Morgan translation. 331pp. 5⅜ x 8½. 20645-9 Pa. $8.95

THE HUMAN FIGURE IN MOTION, Eadweard Muybridge. More than 4,500 stopped-action photos, in action series, showing undraped men, women, children jumping, lying down, throwing, sitting, wrestling, carrying, etc. 390pp. 7⅞ x 10⅝.
20204-6 Clothbd. $25.95

TREES OF THE EASTERN AND CENTRAL UNITED STATES AND CANADA, William M. Harlow. Best one-volume guide to 140 trees. Full descriptions, woodlore, range, etc. Over 600 illustrations. Handy size. 288pp. 4½ x 6⅜.
20395-6 Pa. $5.95

SONGS OF WESTERN BIRDS, Dr. Donald J. Borror. Complete song and call repertoire of 60 western species, including flycatchers, juncoes, cactus wrens, many more—includes fully illustrated booklet.   Cassette and manual 99913-0 $8.95

GROWING AND USING HERBS AND SPICES, Milo Miloradovich. Versatile handbook provides all the information needed for cultivation and use of all the herbs and spices available in North America. 4 illustrations. Index. Glossary. 236pp. 5⅜ x 8½.
25058-X Pa. $6.95

BIG BOOK OF MAZES AND LABYRINTHS, Walter Shepherd. 50 mazes and labyrinths in all—classical, solid, ripple, and more—in one great volume. Perfect inexpensive puzzler for clever youngsters. Full solutions. 112pp. 8⅛ x 11.
22951-3 Pa. $4.95

PIANO TUNING, J. Cree Fischer. Clearest, best book for beginner, amateur. Simple repairs, raising dropped notes, tuning by easy method of flattened fifths. No previous skills needed. 4 illustrations. 201pp. 5⅜ x 8½. 23267-0 Pa. $6.95

A SOURCE BOOK IN THEATRICAL HISTORY, A. M. Nagler. Contemporary observers on acting, directing, make-up, costuming, stage props, machinery, scene design, from Ancient Greece to Chekhov. 611pp. 5⅜ x 8½. 20515-0 Pa. $12.95

THE COMPLETE NONSENSE OF EDWARD LEAR, Edward Lear. All nonsense limericks, zany alphabets, Owl and Pussycat, songs, nonsense botany, etc., illustrated by Lear. Total of 320pp. 5⅜ x 8½. (USO) 20167-8 Pa. $6.95

VICTORIAN PARLOUR POETRY: An Annotated Anthology, Michael R. Turner. 117 gems by Longfellow, Tennyson, Browning, many lesser-known poets. "The Village Blacksmith," "Curfew Must Not Ring Tonight," "Only a Baby Small," dozens more, often difficult to find elsewhere. Index of poets, titles, first lines. xxiii + 325pp. 5⅝ x 8¼. 27044-0 Pa. $8.95

DUBLINERS, James Joyce. Fifteen stories offer vivid, tightly focused observations of the lives of Dublin's poorer classes. At least one, "The Dead," is considered a masterpiece. Reprinted complete and unabridged from standard edition. 160pp. 5³⁄₁₆ x 8¼. 26870-5 Pa. $1.00

THE HAUNTED MONASTERY and THE CHINESE MAZE MURDERS, Robert van Gulik. Two full novels by van Gulik, set in 7th-century China, continue adventures of Judge Dee and his companions. An evil Taoist monastery, seemingly supernatural events; overgrown topiary maze hides strange crimes. 27 illustrations. 328pp. 5⅜ x 8½. 23502-5 Pa. $8.95

THE BOOK OF THE SACRED MAGIC OF ABRAMELIN THE MAGE, translated by S. MacGregor Mathers. Medieval manuscript of ceremonial magic. Basic document in Aleister Crowley, Golden Dawn groups. 268pp. 5⅜ x 8½. 23211-5 Pa. $8.95

NEW RUSSIAN-ENGLISH AND ENGLISH-RUSSIAN DICTIONARY, M. A. O'Brien. This is a remarkably handy Russian dictionary, containing a surprising amount of information, including over 70,000 entries. 366pp. 4½ x 6⅛. 20208-9 Pa. $9.95

HISTORIC HOMES OF THE AMERICAN PRESIDENTS, Second, Revised Edition, Irvin Haas. A traveler's guide to American Presidential homes, most open to the public, depicting and describing homes occupied by every American President from George Washington to George Bush. With visiting hours, admission charges, travel routes. 175 photographs. Index. 160pp. 8¼ x 11. 26751-2 Pa. $11.95

NEW YORK IN THE FORTIES, Andreas Feininger. 162 brilliant photographs by the well-known photographer, formerly with *Life* magazine. Commuters, shoppers, Times Square at night, much else from city at its peak. Captions by John von Hartz. 181pp. 9¼ x 10¾. 23585-8 Pa. $12.95

INDIAN SIGN LANGUAGE, William Tomkins. Over 525 signs developed by Sioux and other tribes. Written instructions and diagrams. Also 290 pictographs. 111pp. 6⅛ x 9¼. 22029-X Pa. $3.95

CATALOG OF DOVER BOOKS

ANATOMY: A Complete Guide for Artists, Joseph Sheppard. A master of figure drawing shows artists how to render human anatomy convincingly. Over 460 illustrations. 224pp. 8⅜ x 11¼. 27279-6 Pa. $10.95

MEDIEVAL CALLIGRAPHY: Its History and Technique, Marc Drogin. Spirited history, comprehensive instruction manual covers 13 styles (ca. 4th century thru 15th). Excellent photographs; directions for duplicating medieval techniques with modern tools. 224pp. 8⅜ x 11¼. 26142-5 Pa. $11.95

DRIED FLOWERS: How to Prepare Them, Sarah Whitlock and Martha Rankin. Complete instructions on how to use silica gel, meal and borax, perlite aggregate, sand and borax, glycerine and water to create attractive permanent flower arrangements. 12 illustrations. 32pp. 5⅜ x 8½. 21802-3 Pa. $1.00

EASY-TO-MAKE BIRD FEEDERS FOR WOODWORKERS, Scott D. Campbell. Detailed, simple-to-use guide for designing, constructing, caring for and using feeders. Text, illustrations for 12 classic and contemporary designs. 96pp. 5⅜ x 8½. 25847-5 Pa. $2.95

SCOTTISH WONDER TALES FROM MYTH AND LEGEND, Donald A. Mackenzie. 16 lively tales tell of giants rumbling down mountainsides, of a magic wand that turns stone pillars into warriors, of gods and goddesses, evil hags, powerful forces and more. 240pp. 5⅜ x 8½. 29677-6 Pa. $6.95

THE HISTORY OF UNDERCLOTHES, C. Willett Cunnington and Phyllis Cunnington. Fascinating, well-documented survey covering six centuries of English undergarments, enhanced with over 100 illustrations: 12th-century laced-up bodice, footed long drawers (1795), 19th-century bustles, l9th-century corsets for men, Victorian "bust improvers," much more. 272pp. 5⅜ x 8¼. 27124-2 Pa. $9.95

ARTS AND CRAFTS FURNITURE: The Complete Brooks Catalog of 1912, Brooks Manufacturing Co. Photos and detailed descriptions of more than 150 now very collectible furniture designs from the Arts and Crafts movement depict davenports, settees, buffets, desks, tables, chairs, bedsteads, dressers and more, all built of solid, quarter-sawed oak. Invaluable for students and enthusiasts of antiques, Americana and the decorative arts. 80pp. 6½ x 9¼. 27471-3 Pa. $7.95

HOW WE INVENTED THE AIRPLANE: An Illustrated History, Orville Wright. Fascinating firsthand account covers early experiments, construction of planes and motors, first flights, much more. Introduction and commentary by Fred C. Kelly. 76 photographs. 96pp. 8¼ x 11. 25662-6 Pa. $8.95

THE ARTS OF THE SAILOR: Knotting, Splicing and Ropework, Hervey Garrett Smith. Indispensable shipboard reference covers tools, basic knots and useful hitches; handsewing and canvas work, more. Over 100 illustrations. Delightful reading for sea lovers. 256pp. 5⅜ x 8½. 26440-8 Pa. $7.95

FRANK LLOYD WRIGHT'S FALLINGWATER: The House and Its History, Second, Revised Edition, Donald Hoffmann. A total revision—both in text and illustrations—of the standard document on Fallingwater, the boldest, most personal architectural statement of Wright's mature years, updated with valuable new material from the recently opened Frank Lloyd Wright Archives. "Fascinating"—*The New York Times*. 116 illustrations. 128pp. 9¼ x 10¾. 27430-6 Pa. $11.95

AUTOBIOGRAPHY: The Story of My Experiments with Truth, Mohandas K. Gandhi. Boyhood, legal studies, purification, the growth of the Satyagraha (nonviolent protest) movement. Critical, inspiring work of the man responsible for the freedom of India. 480pp. 5⅜ x 8½. (USO) 24593-4 Pa. $8.95

CELTIC MYTHS AND LEGENDS, T. W. Rolleston. Masterful retelling of Irish and Welsh stories and tales. Cuchulain, King Arthur, Deirdre, the Grail, many more. First paperback edition. 58 full-page illustrations. 512pp. 5⅜ x 8½. 26507-2 Pa. $9.95

THE PRINCIPLES OF PSYCHOLOGY, William James. Famous long course complete, unabridged. Stream of thought, time perception, memory, experimental methods; great work decades ahead of its time. 94 figures. 1,391pp. 5⅜ x 8½. 2-vol. set.
Vol. I: 20381-6 Pa. $12.95
Vol. II: 20382-4 Pa. $12.95

THE WORLD AS WILL AND REPRESENTATION, Arthur Schopenhauer. Definitive English translation of Schopenhauer's life work, correcting more than 1,000 errors, omissions in earlier translations. Translated by E. F. J. Payne. Total of 1,269pp. 5⅜ x 8½. 2-vol. set.
Vol. 1: 21761-2 Pa. $11.95
Vol. 2: 21762-0 Pa. $11.95

MAGIC AND MYSTERY IN TIBET, Madame Alexandra David-Neel. Experiences among lamas, magicians, sages, sorcerers, Bonpa wizards. A true psychic discovery. 32 illustrations. 321pp. 5⅜ x 8½. (USO) 22682-4 Pa. $8.95

THE EGYPTIAN BOOK OF THE DEAD, E. A. Wallis Budge. Complete reproduction of Ani's papyrus, finest ever found. Full hieroglyphic text, interlinear transliteration, word-for-word translation, smooth translation. 533pp. 6½ x 9¼.
21866-X Pa. $10.95

MATHEMATICS FOR THE NONMATHEMATICIAN, Morris Kline. Detailed, college-level treatment of mathematics in cultural and historical context, with numerous exercises. Recommended Reading Lists. Tables. Numerous figures. 641pp. 5⅜ x 8½.
24823-2 Pa. $11.95

THEORY OF WING SECTIONS: Including a Summary of Airfoil Data, Ira H. Abbott and A. E. von Doenhoff. Concise compilation of subsonic aerodynamic characteristics of NACA wing sections, plus description of theory. 350pp. of tables. 693pp. 5⅜ x 8½. 60586-8 Pa. $14.95

THE RIME OF THE ANCIENT MARINER, Gustave Doré, S. T. Coleridge. Doré's finest work; 34 plates capture moods, subtleties of poem. Flawless full-size reproductions printed on facing pages with authoritative text of poem. "Beautiful. Simply beautiful."–*Publisher's Weekly*. 77pp. 9¼ x 12. 22305-1 Pa. $6.95

NORTH AMERICAN INDIAN DESIGNS FOR ARTISTS AND CRAFTSPEOPLE, Eva Wilson. Over 360 authentic copyright-free designs adapted from Navajo blankets, Hopi pottery, Sioux buffalo hides, more. Geometrics, symbolic figures, plant and animal motifs, etc. 128pp. 8⅜ x 11. (EUK) 25341-4 Pa. $8.95

SCULPTURE: Principles and Practice, Louis Slobodkin. Step-by-step approach to clay, plaster, metals, stone; classical and modern. 253 drawings, photos. 255pp. 8⅛ x 11.
22960-2 Pa. $10.95

PHOTOGRAPHIC SKETCHBOOK OF THE CIVIL WAR, Alexander Gardner. 100 photos taken on field during the Civil War. Famous shots of Manassas Harper's Ferry, Lincoln, Richmond, slave pens, etc. 244pp. 10⅝ x 8¼. 22731-6 Pa. $9.95

FIVE ACRES AND INDEPENDENCE, Maurice G. Kains. Great back-to-the-land classic explains basics of self-sufficient farming. The one book to get. 95 illustrations. 397pp. 5⅜ x 8½. 20974-1 Pa. $7.95

SONGS OF EASTERN BIRDS, Dr. Donald J. Borror. Songs and calls of 60 species most common to eastern U.S.: warblers, woodpeckers, flycatchers, thrushes, larks, many more in high-quality recording. Cassette and manual 99912-2 $8.95

A MODERN HERBAL, Margaret Grieve. Much the fullest, most exact, most useful compilation of herbal material. Gigantic alphabetical encyclopedia, from aconite to zedoary, gives botanical information, medical properties, folklore, economic uses, much else. Indispensable to serious reader. 161 illustrations. 888pp. 6½ x 9¼. 2-vol. set. (USO)
Vol. I: 22798-7 Pa. $9.95
Vol. II: 22799-5 Pa. $9.95

HIDDEN TREASURE MAZE BOOK, Dave Phillips. Solve 34 challenging mazes accompanied by heroic tales of adventure. Evil dragons, people-eating plants, blood-thirsty giants, many more dangerous adversaries lurk at every twist and turn. 34 mazes, stories, solutions. 48pp. 8¼ x 11. 24566-7 Pa. $2.95

LETTERS OF W. A. MOZART, Wolfgang A. Mozart. Remarkable letters show bawdy wit, humor, imagination, musical insights, contemporary musical world; includes some letters from Leopold Mozart. 276pp. 5⅜ x 8½. 22859-2 Pa. $7.95

BASIC PRINCIPLES OF CLASSICAL BALLET, Agrippina Vaganova. Great Russian theoretician, teacher explains methods for teaching classical ballet. 118 illustrations. 175pp. 5⅜ x 8½. 22036-2 Pa. $5.95

THE JUMPING FROG, Mark Twain. Revenge edition. The original story of The Celebrated Jumping Frog of Calaveras County, a hapless French translation, and Twain's hilarious "retranslation" from the French. 12 illustrations. 66pp. 5⅜ x 8½. 22686-7 Pa. $3.95

BEST REMEMBERED POEMS, Martin Gardner (ed.). The 126 poems in this superb collection of 19th- and 20th-century British and American verse range from Shelley's "To a Skylark" to the impassioned "Renascence" of Edna St. Vincent Millay and to Edward Lear's whimsical "The Owl and the Pussycat." 224pp. 5⅜ x 8½. 27165-X Pa. $4.95

COMPLETE SONNETS, William Shakespeare. Over 150 exquisite poems deal with love, friendship, the tyranny of time, beauty's evanescence, death and other themes in language of remarkable power, precision and beauty. Glossary of archaic terms. 80pp. 5³⁄₁₆ x 8¼. 26686-9 Pa. $1.00

BODIES IN A BOOKSHOP, R. T. Campbell. Challenging mystery of blackmail and murder with ingenious plot and superbly drawn characters. In the best tradition of British suspense fiction. 192pp. 5⅜ x 8½. 24720-1 Pa. $6.95

THE WIT AND HUMOR OF OSCAR WILDE, Alvin Redman (ed.). More than 1,000 ripostes, paradoxes, wisecracks: Work is the curse of the drinking classes; I can resist everything except temptation; etc. 258pp. 5⅜ x 8½.   20602-5 Pa. $5.95

SHAKESPEARE LEXICON AND QUOTATION DICTIONARY, Alexander Schmidt. Full definitions, locations, shades of meaning in every word in plays and poems. More than 50,000 exact quotations. 1,485pp. 6½ x 9¼. 2-vol. set.
Vol. 1: 22726-X Pa. $16.95
Vol. 2: 22727-8 Pa. $16.95

SELECTED POEMS, Emily Dickinson. Over 100 best-known, best-loved poems by one of America's foremost poets, reprinted from authoritative early editions. No comparable edition at this price. Index of first lines. 64pp. 5³⁄₁₆ x 8¼.
26466-1 Pa. $1.00

CELEBRATED CASES OF JUDGE DEE (DEE GOONG AN), translated by Robert van Gulik. Authentic 18th-century Chinese detective novel; Dee and associates solve three interlocked cases. Led to van Gulik's own stories with same characters. Extensive introduction. 9 illustrations. 237pp. 5⅜ x 8½.   23337-5 Pa. $6.95

THE MALLEUS MALEFICARUM OF KRAMER AND SPRENGER, translated by Montague Summers. Full text of most important witchhunter's "bible," used by both Catholics and Protestants. 278pp. 6⅝ x 10.   22802-9 Pa. $12.95

SPANISH STORIES/CUENTOS ESPAÑOLES: A Dual-Language Book, Angel Flores (ed.). Unique format offers 13 great stories in Spanish by Cervantes, Borges, others. Faithful English translations on facing pages. 352pp. 5⅜ x 8½.
25399-6 Pa. $8.95

THE CHICAGO WORLD'S FAIR OF 1893: A Photographic Record, Stanley Appelbaum (ed.). 128 rare photos show 200 buildings, Beaux-Arts architecture, Midway, original Ferris Wheel, Edison's kinetoscope, more. Architectural emphasis; full text. 116pp. 8¼ x 11.   23990-X Pa. $9.95

OLD QUEENS, N.Y., IN EARLY PHOTOGRAPHS, Vincent F. Seyfried and William Asadorian. Over 160 rare photographs of Maspeth, Jamaica, Jackson Heights, and other areas. Vintage views of DeWitt Clinton mansion, 1939 World's Fair and more. Captions. 192pp. 8⅞ x 11.   26358-4 Pa. $12.95

CAPTURED BY THE INDIANS: 15 Firsthand Accounts, 1750-1870, Frederick Drimmer. Astounding true historical accounts of grisly torture, bloody conflicts, relentless pursuits, miraculous escapes and more, by people who lived to tell the tale. 384pp. 5⅜ x 8½.   24901-8 Pa. $8.95

THE WORLD'S GREAT SPEECHES, Lewis Copeland and Lawrence W. Lamm (eds.). Vast collection of 278 speeches of Greeks to 1970. Powerful and effective models; unique look at history. 842pp. 5⅜ x 8½.   20468-5 Pa. $14.95

THE BOOK OF THE SWORD, Sir Richard F. Burton. Great Victorian scholar/adventurer's eloquent, erudite history of the "queen of weapons"–from prehistory to early Roman Empire. Evolution and development of early swords, variations (sabre, broadsword, cutlass, scimitar, etc.), much more. 336pp. 6⅛ x 9¼.
25434-8 Pa. $9.95

CATALOG OF DOVER BOOKS

THE INFLUENCE OF SEA POWER UPON HISTORY, 1660–1783, A. T. Mahan. Influential classic of naval history and tactics still used as text in war colleges. First paperback edition. 4 maps. 24 battle plans. 640pp. 5⅜ x 8½. 25509-3 Pa. $12.95

THE STORY OF THE TITANIC AS TOLD BY ITS SURVIVORS, Jack Winocour (ed.). What it was really like. Panic, despair, shocking inefficiency, and a little heroism. More thrilling than any fictional account. 26 illustrations. 320pp. 5⅜ x 8½. 20610-6 Pa. $8.95

FAIRY AND FOLK TALES OF THE IRISH PEASANTRY, William Butler Yeats (ed.). Treasury of 64 tales from the twilight world of Celtic myth and legend: "The Soul Cages," "The Kildare Pooka," "King O'Toole and his Goose," many more. Introduction and Notes by W. B. Yeats. 352pp. 5⅜ x 8½. 26941-8 Pa. $8.95

BUDDHIST MAHAYANA TEXTS, E. B. Cowell and Others (eds.). Superb, accurate translations of basic documents in Mahayana Buddhism, highly important in history of religions. The Buddha-karita of Asvaghosha, Larger Sukhavativyuha, more. 448pp. 5⅜ x 8½. 25552-2 Pa. $9.95

ONE TWO THREE . . . INFINITY: Facts and Speculations of Science, George Gamow. Great physicist's fascinating, readable overview of contemporary science: number theory, relativity, fourth dimension, entropy, genes, atomic structure, much more. 128 illustrations. Index. 352pp. 5⅜ x 8½. 25664-2 Pa. $8.95

ENGINEERING IN HISTORY, Richard Shelton Kirby, et al. Broad, nontechnical survey of history's major technological advances: birth of Greek science, industrial revolution, electricity and applied science, 20th-century automation, much more. 181 illustrations. ". . . excellent . . ."–Isis. Bibliography. vii + 530pp. 5⅜ x 8¼. 26412-2 Pa. $14.95

DALÍ ON MODERN ART: The Cuckolds of Antiquated Modern Art, Salvador Dalí. Influential painter skewers modern art and its practitioners. Outrageous evaluations of Picasso, Cézanne, Turner, more. 15 renderings of paintings discussed. 44 calligraphic decorations by Dalí. 96pp. 5⅜ x 8½. (USO) 29220-7 Pa. $4.95

ANTIQUE PLAYING CARDS: A Pictorial History, Henry René D'Allemagne. Over 900 elaborate, decorative images from rare playing cards (14th–20th centuries): Bacchus, death, dancing dogs, hunting scenes, royal coats of arms, players cheating, much more. 96pp. 9¼ x 12¼. 29265-7 Pa. $11.95

MAKING FURNITURE MASTERPIECES: 30 Projects with Measured Drawings, Franklin H. Gottshall. Step-by-step instructions, illustrations for constructing handsome, useful pieces, among them a Sheraton desk, Chippendale chair, Spanish desk, Queen Anne table and a William and Mary dressing mirror. 224pp. 8⅛ x 11¼. 29338-6 Pa. $13.95

THE FOSSIL BOOK: A Record of Prehistoric Life, Patricia V. Rich et al. Profusely illustrated definitive guide covers everything from single-celled organisms and dinosaurs to birds and mammals and the interplay between climate and man. Over 1,500 illustrations. 760pp. 7½ x 10⅛. 29371-8 Pa. $29.95

Prices subject to change without notice.

Available at your book dealer or write for free catalog to Dept. GI, Dover Publications, Inc., 31 East 2nd St., Mineola, N.Y. 11501. Dover publishes more than 500 books each year on science, elementary and advanced mathematics, biology, music, art, literary history, social sciences and other areas.